collections

Houghton
Mifflin
Harcourt

Close Reader
TEACHER'S GUIDE

GRADE 6

Program Consultants:

Kylene Beers

Martha Hougen

Carol Jago

William L. McBride

Erik Palmer

Lydia Stack

HISTORY

Printed in the U.S.A.

ISBN 978-0-544-08757-6

4 5 6 7 8 9 10   1420   22 21 20 19 18 17 16 15 14

4500470058   B C D E F G

Close Reading— It's a Habit of Mind

By Carol Jago

You read closely every day. Each time you open a bank statement, mull over a new poem in the *New Yorker*, or grade a student paper, you perform a close reading. Often what appears on the page doesn't at first quite make sense. So what do you do? You read the text again, paying attention to places where comprehension broke down, focusing on unfamiliar words or familiar words used in unfamiliar ways. Sometimes you ask a friend for help when the meaning continues to elude you. Close reading isn't a strategy; it's a habit of mind.

In the past we protected students from texts they might find difficult, offering them only "considerate text" that made clear what the main ideas were and simplified dense passages. Unfortunately, college and career-readiness, not to mention the demands of citizenship, requires that students master the art of negotiating a great many inconsiderate texts. We thought we were helping students—trust me, no one has spent more time looking for shorter, easier, funnier things for kids to read than me—but we only succeeded in making the transition to college more difficult. The *Close Reader* offers students various protocols that, once internalized, will allow them to read independently with comprehension the complex texts called for in the Common Core State Standards.

Fortunately, many of these seemingly "inconsiderate" texts are also some of the finest literature ever written. The works of William Shakespeare, Homer, and Ralph Waldo Emerson as well as those of Isabelle Allende, Gwendolyn Brooks, and Ray Bradbury repay the investment of time and trouble taken to read them closely many times over. (So does an accurately read bank statement.)

Cognitive neuroscientist Maryanne Wolf, director of the Center for Reading and Language Research at Tufts University, warns that much of the reading today's young people are doing on the Internet develops a habit of what she calls a state of "continuous partial attention." In *Proust and the Squid: The Story and Science of the Reading Brain* (2007), Wolf describes how the time children spend daily processing a steady stream of online information is actually reshaping the architecture of their brains. As an English teacher, my concern is that while skimming and scanning may be an efficient and effective way to read a Twitter or Facebook feed, it's a very poor way to read poetry. I need my students to develop the ability to read profoundly and introspectively. And independently!

Common Core Anchor Standard #10 for reading states that students must "Read and comprehend complex literary and informational texts independently and proficiently." Working through this *Close Reader* will help your students perform proficiently by developing their independence as readers. As they practice unpacking challenging text for themselves, getting into the habit of rereading, slowing down when the going gets tough, knowing what to do when they meet a new word, students become more confident readers. We can't do the reading for them, not now or later. The *Close Reader* will give you ideas for what to do instead.

Let's make this a nation of close readers.

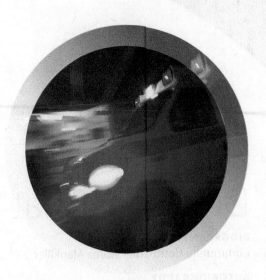

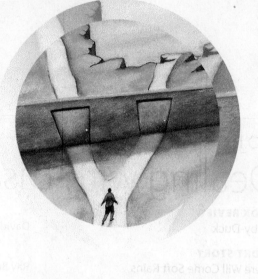

COLLECTION 5
Decisions That Matter

COLLECTION 6
What Tales Tell

How Students Become Close Readers

READING THE TEXTS

Challenging literary and informational texts require students to engage in close reading to understand and appreciate their meanings fully. These texts may have difficult language or complex structures that become clear only with careful study. To fully understand these demanding texts, students need to learn how to read and reread slowly and deliberately.

The Close Reader provides many opportunities to practice close reading. To become close readers, students will:

- read each text in the Close Reader slowly all the way through.
- take time to think about and respond to the READ and REREAD prompts that help focus their reading.
- cite specific textual evidence to support their analysis of the selection.

Your students' goal in close reading is to build useful knowledge as they analyze the author's message and appreciate the author's craft.

Background

This paragraph provides information about the text students are about to read. It helps them understand the context of the selection through additional information about the author, the subject, or the time period in which the text was written.

READ ▶

Questions and specific instructions at the beginning of the selection and on the bottom of the pages will guide students through a close reading of each text.

These questions and instructions:

- refer to specific sections of the text.
- ask students to look for and mark up specific information in the text.
- prompt students to record inferences and text analysis in the side margins.
- help students begin to collect and cite text evidence.

Vocabulary

Critical vocabulary words appear in the margin throughout most selections. Students should consult a print or online dictionary to define the word on their own.

When students see a vocabulary word in the margin, they should:

- write the definition of each word in the margin.
- be sure the definition fits the context of the word as it is used in the text.
- check the definition by substituting it in place of the vocabulary word from the text. The definition should make sense in the context of the selection.

◀ REREAD

To further guide close reading, REREAD questions at the bottom of the page will:

- ask students to focus on a close analysis of a smaller chunk of text.
- prompt students to analyze literary elements and devices, as well as the meaning and structure of informational text.
- help students go back into the text and "read between the lines" to uncover meanings and central ideas.

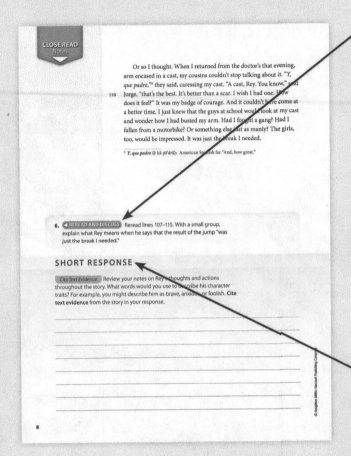

◀ REREAD AND DISCUSS

These prompts encourage students to work with a partner or in a small group to discuss specific events, details, statements, and evidence from the text. These discussions will allow students to acquire and share knowledge about the texts they are reading.

As they engage in these discussions, students should:

- be sure to cite specific text evidence in support of their statements.
- pose questions and integrate their ideas with the ideas of others.
- collaborate to reach a consensus or call attention to evidence that might have been missed or misinterpreted.
- acknowledge the views of others and be ready to modify their own thinking.

SHORT RESPONSE

At the end of each text, students will have an opportunity to sum up their thinking by completing a Short Response. The Short Response represents a place to convey some of the ideas they have developed through close reading of the text.

When students write the Short Response, they should:

- review all margin notes and REREAD responses.
- circle or highlight evidence from the notes that supports their position or point of view.
- clearly state a point of view and support it with reasons.
- cite specific text evidence to support their reasons.

Facing Fear

"Do one thing every day that scares you."

—Eleanor Roosevelt

from The Jumping Tree

Short Story by René Saldaña, Jr.

Why This Text

Students may be more familiar with fiction written from a third-person point of view than they are with first-person narratives. The narrator of "The Jumping Tree" is the story's main character, and readers perceive story events from his perspective. With the help of the close-reading questions, students will make inferences about the narrator and what motivates him based on his description of the events. This close reading will lead students to develop a deeper understanding of the elements of a first-person fictional story.

Background Have students read the background and information about the author. Introduce the selection by pointing out that René Saldaña, Jr. was inspired to write by a love of storytelling, and that this love of storytelling is evident in his writing. Point out that Saldaña is known for his issue-oriented stories about life as he experienced it growing up Latino in South Texas and Georgia.

SETTING A PURPOSE Ask students to pay attention to how the narrator's feelings and actions advance the plot. Do his actions make sense based on their prior knowledge?

Common Core Support

- cite textual evidence to support inferences
- describe how a story's plot unfolds in a series of episodes
- describe how the characters respond or change as the plot moves toward a resolution
- analyze how an author develops the point of view of the narrator in text

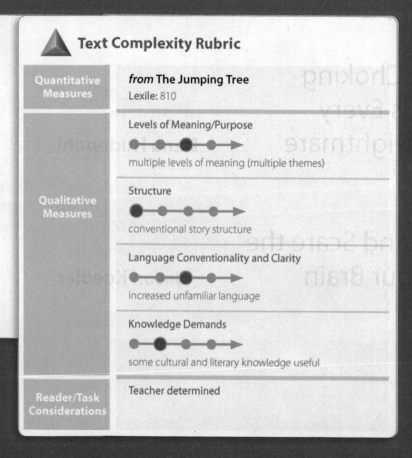

Text Complexity Rubric

Quantitative Measures

from **The Jumping Tree**
Lexile: 810

Qualitative Measures

Levels of Meaning/Purpose

multiple levels of meaning (multiple themes)

Structure

conventional story structure

Language Conventionality and Clarity

increased unfamiliar language

Knowledge Demands

some cultural and literary knowledge useful

Reader/Task Considerations

Teacher determined

Analyze Character

Students should read this story carefully all the way through. Close-reading questions at the bottom of the page will help them focus on a narrator's motivations and interactions. As they read, students should jot down comments or questions about the text in the margins.

WHEN STUDENTS STRUGGLE . . .

To help students analyze the characters in "The Jumping Tree," have them work in small groups to fill out a chart like the one shown below.

CITE TEXT EVIDENCE For practice in analyzing and understanding a character's traits and motivations, ask students to cite text evidence for each point in the chart.

	INFERENCE	EVIDENCE
How does the narrator feel about himself in relation to others?	nervous about cousin's visit	"I didn't know exactly how to entertain him."
	need to impress other kids	"I hadn't done much to get the older kids' respect this summer."
	self-conscious of his age	"I didn't want to do things that were for kids."
What motivates the narrator to act the way he does?	he wants to belong	"I had to prove that I could belong to this group."
	he doesn't want to lose face	"I had to go through with this deal."
	his "manhood" is at stake	"It was a question of manhood."

Background René Saldaña, Jr. *was inspired to become a writer by his grandfather, who was a first-rate storyteller. Saldaña was also motivated by his students when he taught middle school and high school. He told them about the beginnings of his book* The Jumping Tree, *and as they wrote alongside him in class, he was inspired to continue his story.*

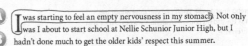

from THE JUMPING TREE

Short Story by René Saldaña, Jr.

CLOSE READ Notes

1. **READ** ▶ As you read lines 1–30, begin to collect and cite text evidence.
   - Circle the phrase that tells how the narrator feels as the story begins.
   - In the margin, explain why the narrator feels this way.
   - Underline the names of the other characters introduced in these lines.

A
B
I was starting to feel an empty nervousness in my stomach. Not only was I about to start school at Nellie Schunior Junior High, but I hadn't done much to get the older kids' respect this summer.

My cousin Jorge, who was a full two years older, was visiting from Mier across the border. This didn't happen too often because we visited my family in Mexico two or three weekends out of the month, and my tío[1] Jorge, Jorge's father, didn't own a car, so Jorge had to wait until my uncle could borrow some transportation. Jorge wouldn't start school for another two weeks, so he wanted to take a vacation in

10 the States.

Odd how just across the border, only some forty-five minutes away, people still walked to work, there was still a milkman, a water truck brought drinking water to each house, and fruit and vegetable **vendors** drove or walked up and down streets selling their wares.

[1] *tío* (tē'ō): Spanish for "uncle."

The narrator is concerned that he will not be able to compete with older kids.

vendors: *people who sell things*

3

---

1. **READ AND CITE TEXT EVIDENCE** Point out that the narrator (the "I" in the story) is also the main character. Since the story events are presented from the narrator's point of view, it's necessary to make inferences about his actions and motivations based on text evidence and your own experience.

A ASK STUDENTS to infer the narrator's character traits by citing specific textual evidence in lines 1–30. Responses may include references to evidence in lines 1–3 and 29–30.

Critical Vocabulary: vendors (line 14) What do the "vendors" indicate about life across the border? *Life there may be slower paced, with individuals selling goods instead of big stores.*

CLOSE READ
Notes

When I'd visit my cousin, he'd always make certain I had a good time. We'd spend hours on end in his father's carpentry shop sawing blocks of wood into rough imitations of cars and planes. We'd shave planks of wood until they felt smooth on the palms of our hands or our cheeks. We'd use the shavings later on for **kindling** or confetti,
20 and we'd dig our fingers into the mountains of sawdust, sometimes as deep as our elbows.

So, when he came up to Peñitas, I wanted to make sure there was always something doing. Since he was older, I didn't want to do things that were for kids, but I didn't know exactly how to entertain him.

At the beginning of summer, Tío Nardo had hammered a few slats of wood to my granddad's mesquite tree in the middle of the backyard, called it a tree house, and we were set. It was just like in *The Brady Bunch*.[2] Only their tree house actually resembled a house, with its walls, windows, roof, and floor. We had to imagine all that. All we
30 had, really, were flat places to sit on. But it was enough for us.

One day after Jorge arrived, Ricky was over, and we came up with a jumping and gymnastics competition. Actually, Ricky came up with the idea because he was good at that stuff. He was always saying,

kindling:

bits of dry wood used to start a fire

---

[2] **The Brady Bunch:** popular TV show of the 1960s and 1970s.

---

2. ◀ REREAD Reread lines 15–24. What can you infer about the narrator's feelings toward his cousin? Underline text evidence that supports your inference.

He seems to get along with his cousin, and they have fun together. He also wants to impress his cousin.

3. READ ▶ As you read lines 31–70, continue to cite textual evidence.

• Underline text that reveals the narrator's thoughts and feelings about jumping.
• Circle details that describe the setting.
• In the margin, explain the narrator's thoughts as his turn to jump approaches.

CLOSE READ
Notes

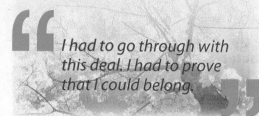
I had to go through with this deal. I had to prove that I could belong.

"Look at this," and he'd tumble, pop a cartwheel, flip backward, or walk on his hands. Once he even walked across the top of a fence like a tightrope walker. Its sharp points didn't seem to bother him.

Ricky explained the rules as we stood under the **mammoth** mesquite. "Okay, we're going to climb the tree and start from there." He pointed to the slat where I normally sat. "Then jump down to that
40 branch there and grab hold." His finger slid across the sky from the plank to a branch that stretched out below it. Easy enough. "Then whoever can do the best trick is the winner and king of the world."

"What do you mean by trick?" asked Jorge.

"You know, flips, swinging back and forth, then letting go, seeing who can land the fanciest."

All this time I'm thinking, *Okay, jump, grab, let go, and pray I land standing. No fancy-schmancy stuff for me. Just do the thing.*

But Jorge was the oldest of us, and the strongest; Ricky was the gymnast; and I was the youngest and the smallest, the one who had
50 something to prove to these guys. I had to go through with this deal. I had to prove that I could belong to this group, could be a man.

"*Orale pues,*"[3] said Jorge. "Let's climb up."

And so we did, hand over hand, foot after foot, until we all reached the top and we **sidled** to the edge of the jumping place. When I saw how far the branch was from this spot, then how far the ground was from that branch, I decided to do the minimum, a jump and release. After all, I was only in the summer after my fifth-grade year. What could they expect?

mammoth:

gigantic, enormous

sidle:

to move sideways

---

[3] **orale pues** (ō-rä′lā pwās): Spanish slang meaning "let's go, then" or "all right, then."

---

2. REREAD AND CITE TEXT EVIDENCE

B **ASK STUDENTS** to suggest one reason for the narrator's insecurity. Students should point out the references to his age in lines 3 and 23.

3. READ AND CITE TEXT EVIDENCE In this section the author reveals the narrator's thoughts directly.

C **ASK STUDENTS** why they think the author uses this technique. Cite a specific example in the text. *Students should cite the italicized text in lines 46–47.*

Critical Vocabulary: kindling (line 19) What does "kindling" suggest about life in Mier? *Students should see that there is little technology.*

Critical Vocabulary: mammoth (line 37) What things might be characterized as "mammoth?" *Students might suggest mountains, skyscrapers, and dinosaurs.*

Critical Vocabulary: sidle (line 54) How does "sidle" help you visualize the setting? *Students might say that visualizing boys standing side by side on a ledge helps you appreciate the danger they face.*

60　Jorge went first. Ricky and I stood back, watching. My Mexican
jumping bean heart was making it hard to concentrate on the task at
hand. Even at this age I knew that people could learn a lot from their
bodies' reactions to a situation: hand over open fire burns: remove
hand immediately; hunger pangs: eat; heart grasping at sides of throat
fighting to get out alongside that morning's breakfast: don't jump!

But, I am Mexican. I could not—strike that—would not back
down. I would do the deed. It was a question of manhood. *¿Macho o
mujeringa? ¡Pues macho!*[4]

Jorge screamed "*¡Aiee!*" and jumped. He swung like a trapeze
artist at the Circus Vargas.[5] I whistled. Then I was one step closer to
70　having to jump.

Ricky stepped up. "We'll see you down there, *primo*,"[6] he said.

"Yeah—down there." I forced a smile.

He jumped and it was like he and the branch were one. The rough
bark of the mesquite melted into a smooth bar in his hands. He

*He cannot
back down,
but he will do
the minimum
and hope for
the best.*

E

---

[4] *¿Macho o mujeringa? ¡Pues macho!* (mä'chō ō mōō'hār-ē'ä): Spanish slang for "Manly or weak and cowardly? Manly!"
[5] **Circus Vargas:** California-based traveling circus.
[6] *primo* (prē'mō): Spanish for "cousin," literally, but also used to mean "pal" or "close friend."

---

4. **◄ REREAD** Reread lines 48–67. Why does the narrator decide to go through with the jump? Make an inference about the narrator based on his reasoning. Support your answer with explicit textual evidence.

*Even though the narrator is nervous about jumping, he wants to
impress Jorge and Ricky. He is jumping to prove to himself and to
Jorge and Ricky that he "could belong to this group" of older kids.*

5. **READ ►** As you read lines 71–115, continue to cite textual evidence.
   • Underline details that convey the narrator's fear as he jumps.
   • Circle details that suggest the narrator has a sense of humor about the events.

6

---

swung forward, let go, twisted, caught the bar again, swung toward
me, flipped, all the while holding on to the branch, released, flipped
in the air once, and stuck the landing. A perfect 10, even from the
Russian judge.

I was next.

80　"*Orale*,"[7] jump!" It sounded like an echo, they were so far away. I
glanced down at them. A big mistake. My stomach was a better
jumper than I because it was already flipping and turning. But I was
at the edge of the board. I'd made a **contract** with myself, for my sake,
signed in blood.

I began to rock back and forth, back and forth, back and forth,
trying for courage.

The time had come. It was my destiny to fly, to live on the very
edge of life, a life James Bond would be jealous of. So I dug my toes
into my tennis shoes, took a deep breath, fought closing my eyes,
90　stretched out my arms and did it.

I saw myself from below somehow. My body like Superman's
flying over Metropolis. The branch growing bigger, closer. Within
reach. All I had to do was to grab hold now. Just let the momentum[8]
carry me toward the branch. The bark, rough on my palms, would be
my safe place. All I had to do was close my fingers around the branch.
Then swing and . . .

But my chubby little soon-to-be-sixth-grade fingers failed me.

I felt the branch slipping from my fingers. And so, like Superman
confronted by kryptonite, I fell.

100　As the ground came closer, I tried to remember my PE coach's
exact advice on how to fall. Had he told his little bunch of munchkins
to roll onto our backs, or to put out our arms and hands? I had only a
split second to make up my mind.

I stretched out my arms to break my fall.

What broke was my left wrist. When I rolled over and looked at
the sky, I knew I had failed.

contract:
agreement

---

[7] *orale:* Spanish slang meaning "let's do it" or "let's go."
[8] **momentum:** the characteristic of a moving body that is caused by its mass and its motion.

7

---

4. **REREAD AND CITE TEXT EVIDENCE** Explain that the narrator sees reasons for and against jumping.

Ⓓ ASK STUDENTS to cite evidence showing that the narrator is trying to talk himself out making the jump. *Students should cite lines 57 and 64.*

5. **READ AND CITE TEXT EVIDENCE** Explain that the author includes Spanish phrases to give the characters authenticity.

Ⓔ ASK STUDENTS to cite evidence showing that the characters are using slang. *Students should cite lines 71, 80, and 108–109.*

Critical Vocabulary: contract (line 83) What are some "contracts" people make with themselves? *Students might suggest eating healthy; learning a language; practicing the piano an hour a day.*

FOR ELL STUDENTS Ask English-speaking volunteers to describe to ELL students the actions referred to in the gymnastics-related expressions. *tumble, pop a cartwheel, flip backward, flips, swinging back and forth, release, and stuck the landing.*

CLOSE READ
Notes

F Or so I thought. When I returned from the doctor's that evening, arm encased in a cast, my cousins couldn't stop talking about it. "*Y, que padre,*"⁹ they said, caressing my cast. "A cast, Rey. You know," said
110 Jorge, "that's the best. It's better than a scar. I wish I had one. How does it feel?" It was my badge of courage. And it couldn't have come at a better time. I just knew that the guys at school would look at my cast and wonder how I had busted my arm. Had I fought a gang? Had I fallen from a motorbike? Or something else just as manly? The girls, too, would be impressed. It was just the break I needed.

⁹ *Y, que padre* (ē kä pä'drä): American Spanish for "And, how great."

6. **◀ REREAD AND DISCUSS** Reread lines 107–115. With a small group, explain what Rey means when he says that the result of the jump "was just the break I needed."

SHORT RESPONSE

Cite Text Evidence Review your notes on Rey's thoughts and actions throughout the story. What words would you use to describe his character traits? For example, you might describe him as brave, anxious, or foolish. **Cite text evidence** from the story in your response.

> Rey is uncertain and anxious as the story begins. He wants to show
> his older cousin a good time, but is not sure how to do that.
> Impressing other people is also important to him. He wants to prove
> that he "could belong to this group, could be a man." He proves to
> himself that he can fit in with older kids by actually jumping.
> Jumping also proves that Rey is brave after all.

8

---

6. **REREAD AND DISCUSS USING TEXT EVIDENCE** The word *break* is used in two ways: the narrator *breaks* his arm, and gets the *break* he needs.

F **ASK STUDENTS** to cite text evidence to show that the narrator thinks it was all worth it. *Students should cite lines 107–115.*

SHORT RESPONSE

Cite Text Evidence Student responses will vary but should use text evidence to support their positions. Students should:

- describe the kind of person Rey is.
- give reasons for Rey's decision.
- cite evidence to show how Rey felt at the end.

DIG DEEPER

1. With the class, return to Question 4, Reread. Have students share their responses to the question.

   ASK STUDENTS what the narrator had to do to convince himself to make the jump in lines 48–67.

   - Have students describe what is happening to the narrator in lines 59–64 and why he takes that as a sign. What can students infer about his resolve at this point in the story?
   - Ask students about the shift in perspective that occurs in lines 65–67. Have them draw conclusions about the significance of being Mexican and what is meant by "a question of manhood." Why do you think the narrator will not allow himself to back down?
   - Ask student why they think the author chose to use Spanish slang in lines 66–67.

2. With the class, return to Question 6, Reread and Discuss. Have students share the results of their discussion.

   ASK STUDENTS to discuss whether or not making the jump was the right thing for Rey to do, and whether it was believable under the circumstances.

   - Have students tell whether they think it would have made a difference to Rey if he had ended up with a worse injury, or if the other kids hadn't been so impressed.
   - Have groups support their ideas using text evidence. Groups should cite evidence in which the author shows that in Latino culture a challenge to one's machismo might seem more devastating than any kind of bodily harm.
   - Have groups analyze what other factors were involved in Rey's decision. Ask whether Rey's age was a factor in his need to prove himself and also played a part in his decision to take a physical risk. Students might present evidence showing that Rey's insecurity led him to believe that his failure to act would be perceived as weakness.

   ASK STUDENTS to return to their Short Response answer and revise it based on the class discussion.

CLOSE READING NOTES

Face Your Fears: Choking Under Pressure Is Every Athlete's Worst Nightmare

Magazine Article by Dana Hudepohl

Why This Text

Students often finish reading a magazine article without a complete understanding of the author's central (or main) ideas. Articles such as this one by Dana Hudepohl may have more than one complex central idea. Guide students to recognize that some central ideas are directly stated, while others are implied. With the help of the close-reading questions, students will cite text evidence to support analysis of ideas that are explicitly stated as well as implied. This close reading will lead students to develop a coherent understanding of the most important ideas and supporting evidence in an informational text.

Background Have students read the background information that defines the meaning of "choking" as used in athletics. Introduce the selection by sharing this definition: "Choking refers to the failure to perform well during a key moment." Point out that as a health writer, Dana Hudepohl uses information about athletes' experiences to discuss the handling of fear and stress effectively while dealing with the pressure to succeed at competitive sports.

SETTING A PURPOSE Ask students to pay close attention to the central ideas in this article and to the text evidence that supports those ideas. How soon does Hudepohl present the article's central idea?

Common Core Support

- cite textual evidence
- determine the central (or main) ideas in a text
- provide a summary of a text distinct from personal opinions and judgments
- analyze the interactions among individuals, events, or ideas in a text

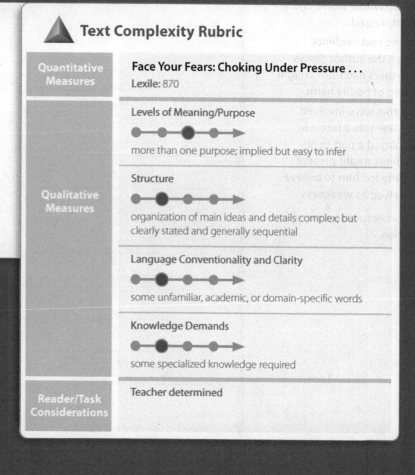

Text Complexity Rubric

Quantitative Measures

Face Your Fears: Choking Under Pressure . . .
Lexile: 870

Qualitative Measures

Levels of Meaning/Purpose
more than one purpose; implied but easy to infer

Structure
organization of main ideas and details complex; but clearly stated and generally sequential

Language Conventionality and Clarity
some unfamiliar, academic, or domain-specific words

Knowledge Demands
some specialized knowledge required

Reader/Task Considerations
Teacher determined

Strategies for CLOSE READING

Cite Evidence

Students should read this article carefully all the way through. Close-reading questions at the bottom of the page will help them focus on a thorough analysis of the central (or main) ideas and on the evidence, including details, facts, statistics, quotations, examples, and anecdotes, that support them. As they read, students should record comments or questions about the text in the side margins.

WHEN STUDENTS STRUGGLE . . .

To practice citing evidence that supports the central ideas of an informational text, students should work in small groups to fill out a two-column chart such as the one shown below.

CITE TEXT EVIDENCE For practice in providing textual evidence from an informational text, ask students to examine the evidence that supports a central (or main) idea.

Central Idea	Text Evidence
It is possible for athletes to overcome their fear and succeed.	Wilkinson faced her fears the night before the final round of diving and was able to move on and win.
	Lindquist overcame her fears by staying focused on the job at hand.
	Hickman doesn't allow fear to overcome her during a race but, like Lindquist, focuses on the job that needs to get done.

Background *In athletics, choking refers to the failure to perform well during a key moment. For example, a golfer who misses an easy putt in the closing moments of a tournament is said to have "choked." In this article from Sports Illustrated for Women, three competitors offer their advice on how to handle fear and stress effectively while dealing with pressure to succeed.*

Face Your Fears: Choking Under Pressure Is Every Athlete's Worst Nightmare

Magazine Article by Dana Hudepohl

CLOSE READ
Notes

1. **READ ▶** As you read lines 1–31, begin to collect and cite text evidence.
   - In the margin, briefly explain what is happening in lines 1–7.
   - Circle the key to Wilkinson's victory and the reaction of the fans (lines 8–12).
   - Underline details that describe Wilkinson's experience at her first international meet.

(A) As she stood on the 10-meter platform at the Sydney Olympics, Laura Wilkinson knew she had to nail her fourth dive to clinch the gold. The pressure was intense: Head-to-head against the toughest divers in the world, she had to be flawless. "In a way I felt I was putting more pressure on myself than I could handle," says Wilkinson, 23. "But I felt like I had nothing to lose. There are more important things than fear."

With that calm attitude, she aced her fourth and fifth dives and won the gold. Her upset victory (she went from fifth to first after
10 three dives) stunned competitors and fans. The key to Wilkinson's victory? Confidence, which was something she had worked on developing in her training.

Laura Wilkinson had to move beyond her fear while diving at the Olympics.

9

1. **READ AND CITE TEXT EVIDENCE** Explain to students that the central idea in the first paragraph (lines 1–7) is not stated directly, but implied. Explain that in order to identify an implied central idea, students need to examine the details to determine what the writer intended.

   (A) ASK STUDENTS to examine the details to infer the central idea of the first paragraph by citing specific textual evidence from lines 1–7. *Responses may include references to evidence in lines 3–7.*

   FOR ELL STUDENTS Explain that *head-to-head* is an idiomatic phrase (or expression). Ask students if they know what it means. How does the idiomatic phrase help suggest the central idea of the paragraph? *Students should see that it expresses the pressure and fear Wilkinson felt, which she knew she had to move beyond in order to win.*

Wilkinson did well on her dives after facing her fears and went on to win the gold medal.

B "When you push away your nerves and refuse to think about them, they come on full force at the most important time: right during the meet," says Wilkinson. So, alone in her hotel room in Sydney, Wilkinson faced her fears the night before the final round of diving. "I let everything hit me: What would happen if I did well? What would happen if I did badly? What am I afraid of?" she recalls.
20 "I was literally shaking just thinking about it, feeling scared and nervous. When I had the courage to stand up to what I was feeling, it didn't seem so bad anymore. I was able to move on."

Wilkinson knows what it's like to get hung up in doubts and anxieties. At her first international meet, she says she was seized by a feeling of near panic. "I was afraid of embarrassing myself and [as a result] I just choked," she says. It took her several meets to get over the experience, which sports psychologists say is not unusual.

"Every player chokes at some point—it's a natural response to competitive stress," says Todd Ryska, a professor of sport psychology at the University of Texas-San Antonio. "Athletes fear it most because
30 of the stigma. No one wants to be the one everyone's talking about in the locker room."

Find Your Focus

D Choking is not a mistake out of nowhere like a shanked[1] golf shot; it's usually the result of misplaced focus. Athletes who avoid choking concentrate on the process (what do I have to do right now?), which is

[1] **shank:** a golf term meaning "to accidentally hit a golf ball with the wrong part of the golf club."

2. ◀ REREAD Reread lines 13–21. Wilkinson says confidence was the key to her Olympic victory. In the margin, list two details that support her statement.

3. READ ▶ As you read lines 32–51, underline the negative effects of fear and stress on Barb Lindquist at her first big meet.

10

---

a positive mental approach. Those who choke tend to dwell on the outcome (what will happen if I don't win?) and its potentially unpleasant **consequences.**

C Letting your attention wander can also lead to trouble. Barb Lindquist, who swam for Stanford from 1987 to 1991, recalls how she
40 felt at her first big meet (the U.S. Open) as she listened to the announcer reciting the accomplishments of her competitors. "I was 16 and I was next to a swimmer that I had read about. I got really flustered by hearing her accomplishments," she says. "I didn't concentrate on my race and was all shaky afterward. I finished last."

Now 31 and a triathlete,[2] Lindquist hasn't had any problems since then. While swimming, she repeats to herself the words "long and strong." On the bike she thinks about her pedal **technique,** and while running she visualizes balloons pulling up her legs to make her feel light. "If you're thinking about each of those things along the way and
50 pushing yourself, you can't really choke," says Lindquist, who finished 2000 ranked seventh in the world.

E Once choking symptoms kick in they're difficult to stop. Libbie Hickman, 35, found this out when she was running the 5,000 meters at the '96 Olympic trials. Hickman led until the last 100 meters, when three runners passed her. "I remember thinking, I'm not doing it. I'm not going to make the team," she says. "As soon as you start focusing on the negative you're dead."

[2] **triathlete:** a person who participates in a three-part athletic contest, which generally includes swimming, biking, and running.

consequences: results

technique: way of accomplishing a task

She focused on negative thoughts and went from first place to finish fourth.

4. ◀ REREAD AND DISCUSS With a small group, discuss the main ideas the writer presents under the heading "Find Your Focus." Include facts and examples in lines 32–37 and the specific experiences of Barb Lindquist in your discussion.

5. READ ▶ Read lines 52–68. In the margin, summarize Hickman's experiences at the 1996 and 2000 Olympic trials.

11

---

2. REREAD AND CITE TEXT EVIDENCE

B **ASK STUDENTS** to examine the way Wilkinson built confidence before her Olympic diving victory. *Students should note that when Wilkinson pushed away her nerves and faced her fears, she was able to gain confidence in her ability to win—and won the gold medal.*

3. READ AND CITE TEXT EVIDENCE Like Laura Wilkinson, Barb Lindquist also knows about the negative effects of fear and stress, and a lack of focus, on a sports competition.

C **ASK STUDENTS** to find and cite the details that also demonstrate the negative effects of pressure and fear on Barb Lindquist at her first big meet. *Students should cite examples from lines 32–51.*

4. REREAD AND DISCUSS USING TEXT EVIDENCE

D **ASK STUDENTS** to appoint a reporter for each group to discuss the main ideas in the section titled "Finding Your Focus." *Students should cite evidence from lines 32–51.*

5. READ AND CITE TEXT EVIDENCE

E **ASK STUDENTS** to read their margin notes to a partner and then write one response that gives an objective summary of Libbie Hickman's experiences at the Olympic trials, using a strong central idea for the summary. *Students should cite evidence from lines 52–68.*

Critical Vocabulary: consequences (line 37) Have students share examples of times when they faced consequences as a result of having done something foolish.

Critical Vocabulary: technique (line 47) Have students explain "technique" as it is used here.

CLOSE READ
Notes

She threw out
her fear and
finished third.

What Hickman learned from that experience helped her at the
2000 trials. "I started getting passed in the last lap, and the fear of
60 coming in fourth again jumped in my head," she says. "But instead of
letting that fear sit there, I threw it out, focused on the job that needed
to be done and saw the finish line." The result: She finished third.

It's Just a Game

F If you have a bad experience, keep it in **perspective**. "Not to
minimize the importance of competition, but it's still only a portion
of life," says Ryska. Your friends and teammates will still accept you
even when you don't perform up to expectations—theirs or yours.
"You have to look forward," says Lindquist. "You only fail in a race
if you haven't learned something from it."

perspective:
viewpoint

6. ◀ **REREAD** Reread lines 63–68. Summarize the important idea
under the heading "It's Just a Game."

It's important to remember that competition is only one part of life.

SHORT RESPONSE

Cite Text Evidence What is the central idea of this article? Review your
reading notes, and **cite text evidence** that supports this idea.

The central idea of this article is that it is possible to overcome fear
and succeed. In the article, all three athletes are unsuccessful until
they find a way to deal with their fear and overcome it.
For example, when Laura Wilkinson "faced her fears" instead of
ignoring them, she was able to "move on" and win. Barb Lindquist
and Libbie Hickman both overcame their fear by learning to focus on
the job at hand instead of the other people competing. As long as
you learn from your failures, you haven't failed at all.

12

---

6. **REREAD AND CITE TEXT EVIDENCE** Ryska warns athletes not
to focus their energies on bad experiences in sports.

F **ASK STUDENTS** to cite evidence that supports the most
important idea in the last section titled "It's Just a Game." *Students*
should cite textual evidence from lines 63–68.

Critical Vocabulary: perspective Ask how "perspective" fits
into Ryska's discussion of learning from a bad experience. *Ryska,*
a professor of sport psychology, wants athletes to maintain a
reasonable outlook after a negative competitive experience.

SHORT RESPONSE

Cite Text Evidence Student responses will vary, but students
should cite text evidence to support the central idea. Students should:

- explain what the central idea is of the article.
- give reasons for their point of view.
- cite specific evidence from the text to support their viewpoint.

TO CHALLENGE STUDENTS . . .

For more context about female athletes in competitive sports,
students can conduct Internet research on other notable female
athletes such as Mia Hamm, Lisa Leslie, or Billie Jean King.

ASK STUDENTS what they have learned about women's
participation in athletics. How has their opinion of female athletes
broadened from their research? *Students should recognize that*
female athletes often face many struggles in order to succeed. Like
male athletes, they have had to learn from their failures in order
to succeed.

DIG DEEPER

With the class, return to Question 4, Reread and Discuss. Have
students share the results of their discussion.

ASK STUDENTS whether they were satisfied with the outcome
of their small-group discussions. Have each group share the main
ideas they found in the section called "Find Your Focus." What
specific evidence from the text did the groups cite to support
their choice of the most important ideas in this section? What
compelling evidence from the article did each group cite about
the specific experiences of Barb Lindquist, who now focuses on
the process (what she has to do right now) In order to win?

- Encourage students to tell whether there was any compelling
  textual evidence cited by group members who did not agree
  with the central ideas found by the group.
- Have groups tell how they used Lindquist's experiences as an
  example of an athlete who has found her focus.
- After students have shared the results of their group's
  discussion, ask whether another group shared any ideas that
  seemed particularly insightful.

ASK STUDENTS to return to their Short Response answer and to
revise it based on the class discussion.

Face Your Fears and Scare the Phobia Out of Your Brain

Magazine Article by Jason Koebler

Why This Text

Students often finish reading a magazine article without a thorough understanding of the author's central (or main) ideas. Articles such as this one by Jason Koebler may have more than one complex central idea. Guide students to recognize that some central ideas are directly stated, while others need to be inferred by analyzing textual evidence. With the help of the close-reading questions, students will determine the central ideas by examining the textual evidence (details, facts, statistics, quotations, examples, and anecdotes). This close reading will lead students to develop a coherent understanding of the most important ideas in an informational text.

Background Have students read the background information that suggests the definition of *phobia* as used in psychology. Introduce the selection by sharing this definition: "A phobia is a marked and persistent fear and avoidance of a particular object or situation." Point out that as a science reporter, Jason Koebler uses scientific information about people's phobias to discuss a new form of therapy.

SETTING A PURPOSE Ask students to pay close attention to the central ideas in this article and to the interactions among individuals, ideas, and events in the text. How soon does Koebler present the article's central idea?

Common Core Support

- cite textual evidence to support what the text says explicitly
- cite textual evidence to support inferences drawn from the text
- determine central (or main) ideas in a text
- analyze central ideas to provide an objective summary of a text

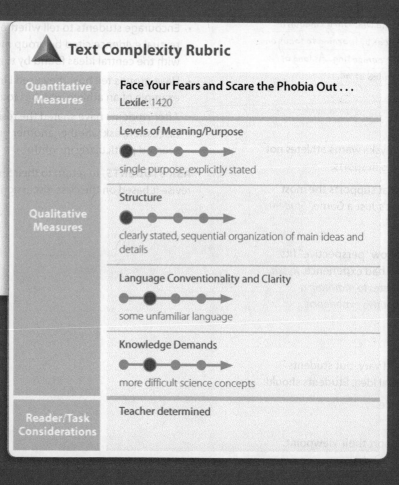

Text Complexity Rubric

	Face Your Fears and Scare the Phobia Out . . .
Quantitative Measures	**Lexile:** 1420

Levels of Meaning/Purpose

single purpose, explicitly stated

Structure

clearly stated, sequential organization of main ideas and details

Language Conventionality and Clarity

some unfamiliar language

Knowledge Demands

more difficult science concepts

| **Reader/Task Considerations** | Teacher determined |

Strategies for CLOSE READING

Determine Central Idea

Students should read this article carefully all the way through. Close-reading questions at the bottom of the page will help them focus on a thorough analysis of the central ideas and the details that support them. As they read, students should record comments or questions about the text in the side margins.

WHEN STUDENTS STRUGGLE . . .

To help students determine the central idea of a text, have them work in small groups to fill out a chart such as the one shown below as they analyze the article.

CITE TEXT EVIDENCE For practice analyzing the central idea of a text, ask students to examine the details and evidence that support the central idea.

Central Idea: Exposure therapy helps eliminate fears and phobias from the brain.

Detail 1: Parts of the brain that produce fear became inactive after people were exposed to the thing they feared.

Detail 2: Exposure therapy changes the way the brain reacts to fear.

Detail 3: Parts of the brain that react to fear remained inactive for at least six months.

Detail 4: After six months, when people were exposed to the thing they feared, they were no longer afraid.

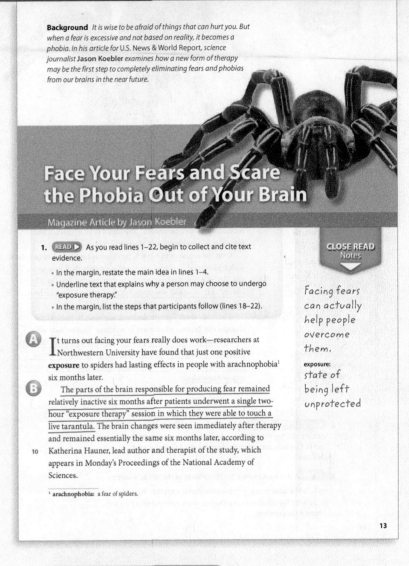

Background *It is wise to be afraid of things that can hurt you. But when a fear is excessive and not based on reality, it becomes a phobia. In his article for U.S. News & World Report, science journalist* **Jason Koebler** *examines how a new form of therapy may be the first step to completely eliminating fears and phobias from our brains in the near future.*

Face Your Fears and Scare the Phobia Out of Your Brain

Magazine Article by Jason Koebler

1. **READ ▷** As you read lines 1–22, begin to collect and cite text evidence.
   - In the margin, restate the main idea in lines 1–4.
   - Underline text that explains why a person may choose to undergo "exposure therapy."
   - In the margin, list the steps that participants follow (lines 18–22).

CLOSE READ Notes

Facing fears can actually help people overcome them.

exposure: *state of being left unprotected*

(A) It turns out facing your fears really does work—researchers at Northwestern University have found that just one positive **exposure** to spiders had lasting effects in people with arachnophobia[1] six months later.

(B) The parts of the brain responsible for producing fear remained relatively inactive six months after patients underwent a single two-hour "exposure therapy" session in which they were able to touch a live tarantula. The brain changes were seen immediately after therapy and remained essentially the same six months later, according to
10 Katherina Hauner, lead author and therapist of the study, which appears in Monday's Proceedings of the National Academy of Sciences.

[1] **arachnophobia:** a fear of spiders.

13

---

1. **READ AND CITE TEXT EVIDENCE** Explain that the central idea in this first paragraph is stated directly.

(A) ASK STUDENTS to read their margin notes to a partner and then write one response that best states the central (or main) idea of the first paragraph, citing textual evidence to support it. *Responses will include references to evidence in lines 1–4.*

Critical Vocabulary: exposure (line 3) Have students explain *exposure* as it is used here. Why is the word used to describe this type of therapy? *This therapy exposes people to the object or situation that they fear.*

FOR ELL STUDENTS Explain that *It turns out (that)* (line 1) is an idiomatic phase (or expression). Ask students what it means. *It means "to be found to be something."*

ASK STUDENTS to look for other idiomatic phrases (or expressions) and cite them in the margin.

CLOSE READ
Notes

Touch a live
tarantula
1. with a
   paintbrush
2. with a
   gloved hand
3. with a bare
   hand

"These people had been clinically afraid of spiders since childhood . . . they'd have to leave the house if they thought there was a spider inside," she says. According to the NIH, about 8 percent of people have a "specific phobia," considered to be a "marked and persistent fear and avoidance of a specific object or situation."

Over the course of two hours, participants touched a live tarantula with a paintbrush, a gloved hand, and eventually their bare hand. "It's 20 this idea that you slowly approach the thing you're afraid of. They learned that the spider was predictable and controllable, and by that time, they feel like it's not a spider anymore."

D The study sheds light on the brain responses to fear and the changes that happen when a fear is overcome. Immediately after therapy, activity in the participants' amygdalas, the part of the brain believed to be responsible for fear responses, remained relatively **dormant** and stayed that way six months later when participants were exposed to spiders.

dormant:
inactive

2. **◄ REREAD AND DISCUSS** Reread lines 1–22. With a small group, discuss whether the evidence convinces you that exposure therapy works. Cite facts and examples from the text to support your opinions.

3. **READ ▶** As you read lines 23–35, continue to cite textual evidence.
   • Underline what happens in the brain during exposure therapy.
   • Circle the fears that exposure therapy treats best and underline the fears it does not treat.

14

CLOSE READ
Notes

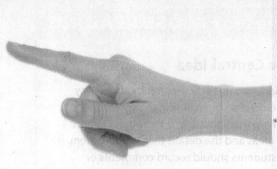

C Hauner says the study proves that exposure therapy works and 30 can potentially be used to develop new treatment methods for people with extreme phobias. She says a similar method can be used on people with fears of confined spaces, heights, flying, blood, and more.

"It has to be an **innocuous** object or situation—it's not a phobia if you're scared of sharks and don't want to go in shark-infested water," she says. "That's called being safe."

innocuous:
not causing
harm or
offense

4. **◄ REREAD** Reread lines 23–35. Summarize the study in lines 23–28 in your own words.
Exposure therapy changes the way the brain reacts to fear, and that change lasts for at least six months.

5. **READ ▶** As you read lines 36–42, underline text that explains future uses of exposure therapy.

15

---

2. **REREAD AND DISCUSS USING TEXT EVIDENCE**

B **ASK STUDENTS** to appoint a reporter for each group to cite specific textual evidence, including scientific facts and examples, to support their opinions about the effectiveness of exposure therapy. *Students should cite evidence from lines 1–22.*

3. **READ AND CITE TEXT EVIDENCE**

C **ASK STUDENTS** to locate and cite specific examples of the fears that exposure therapy treats successfully as well as the fears it doesn't treat. *Students should cite specific textual examples from lines 29–35.*

Critical Vocabulary: dormant (line 27) Ask how *dormant* fits into Koebler's discussion of the brain's responses to fear and the changes that occur when a fear is overcome. *Right after exposure therapy, the part of the brain responsible for fear responses remained inactive for at least six months.*

4. **REREAD AND CITE TEXT EVIDENCE**

D **ASK STUDENTS** to cite textual evidence (scientific facts and examples) that supports the main idea in a brief summary of the study. *Students should cite specific evidence from lines 23–28.*

5. **READ AND CITE TEXT EVIDENCE**

E **ASK STUDENTS** to cite textual evidence, based on the inferences and conclusions that therapists have drawn from the study, to explain possible future uses of exposure therapy. *Students should cite evidence from lines 36–42.*

Critical Vocabulary: innocuous (line 33) Have students explain **innocuous** as it is used here. Encourage them to cite innocuous objects or situations. *Students should be able to explain harmless objects or situations that can cause phobias, such as fear of thunder or of Friday the 13th, that are inoccuous in reality.*

CLOSE READ
Notes

 E **F** In the near future, therapists might be able to inhibit the part of the brain responsible for fear or stimulate the region of the brain responsible for blocking fear in order to begin new therapies.

stimulate:
excite

40 "There's already techniques we use to **stimulate** regions of the brain to treat depression and OCD,"[2] she says. "It's not too far off in the future that we can use these techniques to treat other types of disorders."

[2] **OCD:** OCD, or obsessive-compulsive disorder, is an anxiety disorder characterized by intrusive thoughts and repetitive behaviors.

6. **◀ REREAD** Reread lines 36–42. What is the main idea of this section?

In the future, exposure therapy might be used to treat different problems.

SHORT RESPONSE

Cite Text Evidence Which information from the text most convinces you of the effectiveness of exposure therapy? **Cite text evidence** with specific facts and examples from the text.

The Northwestern University study provided the most convincing evidence about the effectiveness of exposure therapy. During the study, participants overcame a fear of spiders by learning that they are "predictable" and "controllable." This proves that exposure therapy works for people with specific phobias. The study also indicates that exposure therapy is effective in the long term. Participants were not afraid of spiders six months after the study.

16

6. REREAD AND CITE TEXT EVIDENCE

F **ASK STUDENTS** to cite textual evidence to support the central idea. *Support for the central idea is that exposure therapy might help therapists to find new ways to treat phobias or other types of psychological problems.*

Critical Vocabulary: stimulate (line 39) Have students share their definitions of *stimulate*. Ask how *stimulate* fits into the scientific discussion. *Koebler wants to share the study's findings that stimulating areas of the brain can treat certain disorders.*

SHORT RESPONSE

Cite Text Evidence Students should:

- explain whether or not they were convinced of the effectiveness of exposure therapy.
- give reasons for their point of view.
- cite specific evidence from the text to support their viewpoint.

TO CHALLENGE STUDENTS . . .

For more context about fears and phobia, students can view the video titled "Fear" in their eBooks.

ASK STUDENTS to compare the aspects of fear that the scientists in the video are researching with the aspects of fear the scientists in the article are researching. *Students should note that the scientists in the video are concerned with discovering why human beings are afraid while the scientists in the article are researching how people can overcome their fears. Ask students to cite evidence to support their explanation.*

DIG DEEPER

With the class, return to Question 2, Reread and Discuss. Have students share the results of their discussion.

ASK STUDENTS whether they were satisfied with the outcome of their small-group discussions. Have each group share what the majority opinion was of the group. What persuasive evidence from the text did the group cite to support this opinion?

- Encourage students to tell whether there was any convincing evidence cited by group members holding the minority opinion about the effectiveness of exposure therapy. If so, why didn't it sway the group's opinion?

- Have groups explain whether or not they found sufficient persuasive evidence to support their point of view. Did everyone agree as to what made the evidence sufficient? How did the group resolve any differences of opinion?

- After groups have shared the results of their group discussion, ask whether another group shared any findings that persuaded them to change their opinion.

ASK STUDENTS to return to their Short Response answer to revise it, adding essential facts and examples, or deleting unnecessary details, based on the class discussion.

Animal Intelligence

Animal Intelligence

"Each species, however inconspicuous and humble, . . . is a masterpiece."

—Edward O. Wilson

SHORT STORY
The Pod
Maureen Crane Wartski

INFORMATIONAL TEXT
Can Animals Feel and Think?
DeShawn Jones

SCIENCE WRITING
Bats!
Mary Kay Carson

The Pod

Short Story by Maureen Crane Wartski

Why This Text

Students often read a short story without understanding how the elements of a story interact. The characters may respond to the events of the plot and change as the plot moves forward. With the help of the close-reading questions, students will recognize how the characters respond or change as the plot moves toward a resolution of the conflict. This close reading will also guide students to understand how the author develops the narrator's point of view.

Background Have students read the background and the information about the author. Tell students that Maureen Crane Wartski is a naturalized American citizen who was born in Japan. The author of many novels for children and young adults, she is also an expert watercolorist, blending storytelling and art in her young-adult novels and in the quilts she makes.

SETTING A PURPOSE Ask students to pay close attention to how the plot unfolds in a series of episodes and how a main character responds or changes as the plot moves toward a resolution. How soon into the story can students begin to identify the conflict?

Common Core Support

- cite textual evidence
- describe how a story's plot unfolds in a series of episodes (or events)
- describe how a character responds or changes as the plot moves toward a resolution
- explain how an author develops the point of view of the narrator

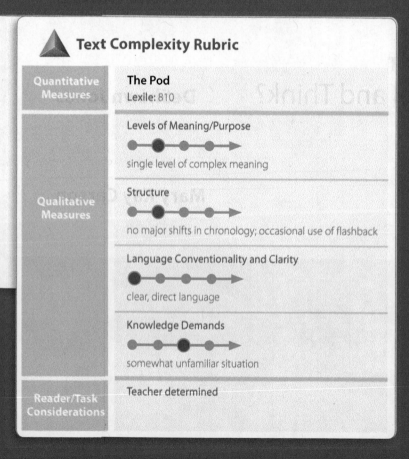

Text Complexity Rubric

Quantitative Measures	**The Pod** Lexile: 810
Qualitative Measures	Levels of Meaning/Purpose — single level of complex meaning
	Structure — no major shifts in chronology; occasional use of flashback
	Language Conventionality and Clarity — clear, direct language
	Knowledge Demands — somewhat unfamiliar situation
Reader/Task Considerations	Teacher determined

Describe Characters' Responses

Students should read this short story carefully all the way through. Close-reading questions at the bottom of the page will help them analyze how a main character responds or changes as the plot moves toward a resolution. As they read, students should record comments or questions about the text in the side margins.

WHEN STUDENTS STRUGGLE . . .

To help students understand the way a character responds or changes as the plot moves toward a resolution, have them work in a small group to fill out a story map, such as the one shown below, as they analyze the story.

CITE TEXT EVIDENCE The power of a story such as this one comes from a main character's response to events in the plot. For practice in tracking how the character changes as the action moves forward, have students complete the story map.

> *Setting: Jesse's house; a road by the ocean*

> *Major Characters: Jesse and his cousin Pete*
>
> *Minor Characters: Jesse's mother, the dolphin, the dolphin's pod*

> *Plot/Problem: Jesse is annoyed at his cousin Pete for his boring lectures about "fish" (marine mammals), but then Jesse is faced with having to rescue a dolphin.*

> *Event 1:*
> *Jesse leaves the house to escape Pete's dull lecture and his family's pity.*

> *Event 2:*
> *Jesse finds a wounded, stranded dolphin and tries to rescue it.*

> *Event 3:*
> *Jesse tries to call Pete for help. He wishes he had paid more attention.*

> *Outcome: As he remembers Pete's lecture, Jesse saves the dolphin and returns him to his pod. Jesse realizes he needs to return to his own family.*

Background Maureen Crane Wartski *was born in Ashiya, Japan, in 1940. Her European and Asian heritage and her deep connection with nature have strongly influenced her writing. In addition, Wartski is an accomplished artist. Like her writing, her watercolors often portray the natural world. Here she writes about dolphins, which, like whales, travel together in groups called "pods."*

The Pod

Short Story by Maureen Crane Wartski

CLOSE READ Notes

1. **READ ▶** As you read lines 1–19, begin to collect and cite text evidence.

- Circle the question at the beginning of the story.
- In the margin, explain how the question helps you understand how Jesse feels about Pete at the beginning of the story.
- Underline text that explains the reasons for Jesse's feelings about Pete and the rest of his family.

A (Couldn't Pete talk about anything but *fish*?)

Jesse Waring tried to block his cousin's voice but there was no escape.

"Dolphins aren't fish, they're mammals," Pete was lecturing. "They look big and tough, but they can get stressed or scared, like the stranded dolphin we rescued. . . ."

"Jesse?" His mother was standing beside him, her eyes full of concern. **B** His parents were always worrying about him these days, Jesse thought, **irritably**, and the other relatives were just as bad.

10 *Poor Jesse, it's a shame about the accident. He used to be a great athlete. . . . Even when they didn't talk to him, he could feel their pitying thoughts.*

"Can you go to the store for me?" his mother was saying. "We've run out of milk. That is," she added quickly, "if you're not too tired. . . ."

It shows that Jesse is annoyed at Pete and is sick of hearing about "fish."

irritably: *showing annoyance*

19

---

1. **READ AND CITE TEXT EVIDENCE** Explain to students that Wartski begins the story by describing the main characters, Jesse and his cousin Pete, and by establishing the conflict of the plot.

A **ASK STUDENTS** to determine how Jesse feels about Pete and the rest of his family since his accident by examining Jesse's thoughts, words, and actions and by citing specific textual evidence in lines 1–19. *Responses may include specific references to evidence in lines 1–3, 8–12, and 16–19.*

Critical Vocabulary: irritably (line 9) Have students share their definitions of *irritably*. Why does Wartsky use the word to describe Jesse's response to his family's concern about him? *Students should point out that Jesse is annoyed by his parents' (and his other relatives') worried looks and attitude toward him since his accident.*

"...And I want to make sure to visit the Cape Cod Stranding Network." Pete was droning on. "They have a hotline, and they do great work...."

Yada, yada, yada. "Sure Mom," Jess said. *Anything to get away from Pete's lectures and all those pitying eyes.*

20   He snatched up car keys from the table in the entryway, grabbing his windbreaker as he limped out the door. Once outside, he wished he'd brought his parka—the wind had an icy sting—but he wasn't going back into the house.

C   He'd always enjoyed the annual Waring family reunion, when cousins, uncles and aunts from all over the country got together and rented a house on New England's Cape Cod, but this March was different. It was the first time the clan had gathered since the accident.

D   Jesse didn't want to think about how a man driving a pickup had jumped a red light, slamming into his car and fracturing his legs. 30 Until then Jesse had been the star of the school soccer team, certain of an athletic scholarship.

   "Not anymore," he muttered, then frowned as he realized he'd passed the store. Well, OK, there was a convenience store about 30 miles away, and the drive would give him some needed alone time.

   At first, the silence was great.

   But as Jesse drove on the road that wound beside the ocean, he kept thinking how his future had been smashed along with his legs. Pep talks that people gave him made it worse. He was a cripple, and

Margin notes left:

He no longer enjoys the family reunions.

He is no longer star of the soccer team and cannot get an athletic scholarship.

He feels that his future is smashed and that he is a cripple.

---

2. ◀ **REREAD** Reread lines 7–14. How does Jesse respond to the accident? Explain what this tells you about his character. Support your answer with explicit textual evidence.

Jesse responds with anger and frustration. He seems annoyed by his mother and Pete and resents what he sees as their pity.

3. **READ** ▶ As you read lines 20–40, continue to cite textual evidence.
- Underline the text that shows what Jesse was like before the accident.
- Note in the margin how this event has changed him.

20

---

40 he knew it. These days Jesse always felt as if there was a tight, hard knot in his chest.

   On **impulse**, he turned the wheel, pulling into an empty parking lot that faced the water. He got out and limped down some stairs. Except for screeching seagulls and a few scattered rocks, the beach was deserted.

   Suddenly, Jesse tensed. *That rock ... did it move?* He took a step closer and saw that it was no rock.

   The dolphin wasn't very big, not even four feet long. When Jesse hobbled over, the big fish ... *mammal, according to Pete* ... rolled an eye at him. How long had it been there? It was breathing, but its sides 50 were heaving painfully.

E **F** Fragments of Pete's endless **monologue** came back to him. His cousin had said that a dolphin's rib structure wasn't built to protect it on land. The body weight of this creature was slowly compressing its vital organs, and if it didn't get back into the water soon, it could die. It was going to low tide and the waves seemed far away. The best thing to do was to call Pete, who would know what to do. Jesse reached for his cell phone.

   It wasn't there. He'd left it in the pocket of his parka! He could drive home and get Pete, but that would mean leaving the dolphin.

Margin notes right:

impulse:
a sudden urge

monologue:
a long speech

He realizes that Pete's knowledge might be important.

---

4. ◀ **REREAD** As you reread lines 28–35, compare Jesse's life before and after the accident. Why do you think he misses the convenience store? Support your answer with explicit textual evidence.

Jesse was a soccer star before the accident and always liked seeing family. Now he feels that his old life is over. He is so distracted that he drives past the store.

5. **READ** ▶ As you read lines 41–61, continue to cite textual evidence.
- Underline the text that tells what Jesse thinks about immediately after he sees the stranded dolphin.
- Circle the text that shows how Jesse's feelings toward Pete have changed, and restate the change in the margin.

21

---

2. **REREAD AND CITE TEXT EVIDENCE**

B **ASK STUDENTS** to cite explicit textual evidence that shows how Jesse's response to his accident reveals his character and shows how he has changed since the crash. *Students should cite specific evidence from lines 8–12.*

3. **READ AND CITE TEXT EVIDENCE**

C **ASK STUDENTS** to read their margin notes to a partner and then write one response that best states how Jesse has changed since his accident, citing specific textual evidence. *Students should cite examples in lines 24–27, 30–31, and 36–40.*

FOR ELL STUDENTS Review the meaning of the phrasal verb **pull into** (line 41), pointing out that in the context of the story, it means "to put the car in a parking space." Point out the differences in the meaning of the verb with and without the preposition.

4. **REREAD AND CITE TEXT EVIDENCE**

D **ASK STUDENTS** to evaluate the significance of the event in which Jesse drives past the convenience store. What does it show about Jesse's state of mind since the accident? *Students should cite evidence from lines 28–31 and 32–34.*

5. **READ AND CITE TEXT EVIDENCE**

E **ASK STUDENTS** to read their margin notes to a partner and then write one response that shows why Jesse's feelings toward Pete have changed, citing specific textual evidence. *Students should cite examples in lines 51–56 and 58–59.*

Critical Vocabulary: impulse (line 41) Have students give examples of instances when someone has followed an impulse. *Students should cite times when they have seen someone act rashly.*

Critical Vocabulary: monologue (line 51) Ask students to share definitions of *monologue* and to use it in a sentence.

60 Would it be alive when he got back? He knew nothing about this creature except that it was helpless.

(G) The dolphin's eyes rolled again, and Jesse felt a sudden jolt of **empathy**.

It looked as scared as he had felt when they'd wheeled him into the emergency room that afternoon.

(H) "Hey, Bud, . . ." Jesse knelt down beside the dolphin. "OK, I just can't leave you here to die. But how do I get you back into the water?"

Even if he managed to drag this creature that weighed — what? maybe 75 pounds? back into the water, the coarse sand might damage
70 its skin. Jesse looked helplessly toward the gray ocean and was surprised to see dark shapes **arcing** out of the waves. A pod[1]—Pete's word—was out there.

"I think your family's waiting for you, Bud." Carefully, Jesse reached out and patted the dolphin. Was it his imagination that his touch made the dolphin calmer?

(I) Jesse didn't want to waste time thinking about that. He was trying to remember what Pete had said about how, when he'd helped rescue a stranded dolphin, he had put the creature on a sort of blanket sling and carried that **contraption** down to the water. Well, he didn't
80 have a blanket handy, so his windbreaker would have to do.

Carefully, Jesse scooped a hollow in the soft sand under the dolphin's head, then eased part of the windbreaker under it. He was streaming with sweat by the time he managed to maneuver as much of the dolphin as possible onto its makeshift "blanket," then began to drag the dolphin toward the water.

[1] pod: a school (or family) of dolphins or other sea mammals.

empathy:
identifying with someone else's feelings or situation

arcing:
making a curved path

contraption:
a device

6. **◀ REREAD AND DISCUSS** *Irony* is a contrast between what is expected and what actually happens. With a small group, discuss how Jesse's feelings about Pete's lectures may be changing. What makes this change surprising?

7. **READ ▶** As you read lines 62–75, continue to cite textual evidence.
- Underline the text that demonstrates how Jesse continues to benefit from Pete's lecture as he cares for the dolphin.
- Circle the text that shows that Jesse is comparing himself to the dolphin.

22

Twice, his legs buckled under him, tumbling him backward onto the sand, but he kept going until water was lapping around his ankles.

"Almost there, Bud," Jesse gritted.

As Jesse waded knee-deep into the water, the dolphin made some
90 kind of noise and then began to swim.

"Woo hoo!" Jesse yelled, then yelped in **dismay**. The dolphin was swimming back toward the shore.

What was wrong with the crazy creature? Pete's voice began to drone in Jesse's mind again, recounting his own dolphin rescue; "*The dolphin was **disoriented**. It kept heading for the shore. We had to guide it back into the deep water. . . .*"

Jesse waded deeper, past the breakers. Icy waves broke against him as he tried to head off the young dolphin. When he'd finally managed that, it wouldn't turn. He wished he had paid more attention to Pete's
100 lecture, but wishing never helped.

(J) Waves sent freezing spumes into his face. "Bud, you've got to save yourself." Jesse gritted through chattering teeth. "Nobody's going to do it for you. If you give up, you're finished. . . ."

Suddenly, as if it had at last understood, the young dolphin turned toward deeper water and began to swim toward the pod. Waiting dolphins arced nearer as if in welcome, and watching them, Jess thought of his own family. They'd be worried because he'd been gone so long.

My pod, he thought.

dismay:
feeling alarmed

disoriented:
confused

It is ironic because in the past he has thought Pete's lectures were boring.

8. **◀ REREAD** Reread lines 66–75. What does Jesse do to care for the dolphin? How do his actions show that Jesse is changing as the story moves forward? Support your answer with explicit textual evidence.

Jesse does not want to leave the stranded dolphin alone, and he tries to make it feel calmer. He tries to figure out how to get the animal back into the water. Jesse's empathy for the dolphin helps him lose his anger and take responsibility for the dolphin and himself.

9. **READ ▶** As you read lines 76–117, continue to cite textual evidence.
- Underline the actions Jesse takes to get the dolphin back into the water.
- In the margin, tell why it is ironic that Jesse remembers Pete's words.

23

6. **REREAD AND DISCUSS USING TEXT EVIDENCE**

(F) ASK STUDENTS to appoint a reporter for each group to cite specific textual evidence that shows irony in the text and how Jesse's point of view toward Pete and his lectures may be changing. *Students should cite specific evidence from lines 51–57 and 58–59.*

7. **READ AND CITE TEXT EVIDENCE**

(G) ASK STUDENTS to cite specific textual evidence to show that Jesse is beginning to relate to the wounded, frightened dolphin and its situation. *Students should cite evidence from lines 62–65 and 73–75.*

Critical Vocabulary: empathy (line 63), **arcing** (line 71), and **contraption** (line 79) Have students share their definitions of the words and use each in a sentence. How does the use of *empathy* lead you to realize that Jesse is beginning to relate to the dolphin?

8. **REREAD AND CITE TEXT EVIDENCE**

(H) ASK STUDENTS to cite textual evidence that shows how Jesse's actions toward the dolphin indicate a change in his character as the plot moves toward a resolution. *Jesse's response to the dolphin's distress suggests that his feelings toward his family, and himself, have changed. Students should cite evidence in lines 66–67, 68–72, and 73–75.*

9. **READ AND CITE TEXT EVIDENCE**

(I) ASK STUDENTS to read their margin notes to a partner, and then create one response that best represents the ironic situation posed by Jesse's attempt to remember Pete's words. *Students should cite textual evidence in lines 76–85, 93–100, and 101–105.*

Critical Vocabulary: dismay (line 91) and **disoriented** (line 95) Ask students to define *dismay* and *disoriented*. Point out that *dis-* is often used as a prefix, meaning "not" or "away from," as in *disoriented*. Have them cite other words with *dis-*.

CLOSE READ
Notes

110   He was freezing as he limped back to his car, but he was grinning, and he was happier than he'd been in a long while.

    He was going to drive to the nearest store and call Pete, who would probably contact the Cape Cod Stranding Network hotline that he'd been talking about. The CCSN would make sure that Bud didn't strand again.

    "But that's not going to happen anyway," Jesse said aloud.

    He had a feeling the young dolphin was finally on the right track.

---

10. ◀ REREAD As you reread lines 101–117, explain why what Jesse says to the dolphin could really be applied to himself. To whom might Jesse be referring when he says that the young dolphin is "on the right track"?

Like the dolphin, Jesse has to save himself and change his attitude. He can't give up. When he says that the dolphin is "on the right track," he is probably also referring to himself.

SHORT RESPONSE

Cite Text Evidence Explain how events in the story change Jesse's feelings about his cousin Pete. How does this response to Pete show that Jesse himself has changed as he struggled to rescue the stranded dolphin? **Cite text evidence** to support your response.

At the beginning of the story, Jesse is tired of listening to Pete's lectures about sea mammals, which Jesse calls "fish." However, when Jesse encounters the stranded dolphin, he tries to call Pete for advice, something he would not have done before. He tries to remember what Pete has said about rescuing dolphins. As he remembers Pete's lecture, he realizes that he will have to make a makeshift blanket to carry the dolphin to the ocean, and he will have to take the dolphin into deep water. By remembering Pete's words, Jesse saves the dolphin—and himself—in the process.

24

---

10. REREAD AND CITE TEXT EVIDENCE

J **ASK STUDENTS** to cite specific textual evidence and line numbers to support the idea that Jesse's identification with the dolphin is complete. By ending the story with Jesse's perception that "the young dolphin was finally on the right track," students should infer that Jesse could be referring to himself. *Students should cite evidence from lines 101–103, 104–109, and 110–117.*

SHORT RESPONSE

Cite Text Evidence Student responses will vary, but students should cite evidence from the text to support their ideas. Students should:

- explain how Jesse's response to Pete changes as the plot moves toward the resolution of the conflict.
- give reasons for their point of view.
- cite specific evidence from the text to track how the narrator's point of view toward Jesse changes.

TO CHALLENGE STUDENTS . . .

For more context about dolphins, students can conduct research online or in the library on these fascinating creatures.

ASK STUDENTS to discover more information about the intelligence of dolphins by writing a research report. Some research topics about dolphins might include:

- how dolphins communicate
- fascinating facts about dolphins, whales, and porpoises
- swimming with dolphins

With the class, discuss these elements of a research report after students have chosen a topic.

PLAN YOUR RESEARCH

- Write questions about your topic.
- Research your topic and take notes.
- Organize your notes.
- Write an outline based on your notes.

WRITE YOUR REPORT

- Keep your purpose and audience in mind.
- Write a first draft.
- Revise your report, and proofread it.
- Check that your bibliography is correct.

PUBLISH AND SHARE

- Make a final copy of your report.
- Publish and share it.

ASK STUDENTS what they hope to discover about dolphins as they research their report. How is the information they find similar to, yet different from, the facts in "The Pod"?

DIG DEEPER

With the class, return to Question 6, Reread and Discuss. Have students share the results of their discussion.

ASK STUDENTS whether they were pleased with the outcome of the small-group discussions. Have each group share the details of its discussion about irony in "The Pod." How did each group define the term *irony* in the context of the story? What made the situation in the story ironic? *Students should recognize that the situation in which Jesse finds himself with the stranded dolphin is ironic because what is expected to happen does not actually happen, in a surprising twist of the plot. Jesse had not cared about what his cousin Pete had to say about dolphins or their rescue before, and now he is faced with having to save one that is stranded. Jesse's feelings toward his cousin Pete are also ironic because he begins to realize that he should have paid attention to Pete's lectures about "fish" (really, marine mammals) as he tries hard to remember Pete's words about how to rescue a dolphin.*

Encourage groups to share any other ideas they may have had about irony in the story. For example, is there a discrepancy between what seems to be and what is? What textual evidence did group members cite to support the idea that the narrator's point of view toward Jesse changed too abruptly?

- Guide each group to tell how it decided on the ironic details of the story. Were there any group members who did not agree with the decision of the group? If so, how did the group resolve any conflicts or differences of opinion?
- After groups have shared the results of their discussion, ask whether another group had shared any ideas they wish they had thought of.

ASK STUDENTS to return to their Short Response answer and to revise it based on the class discussion about the conflict between Jesse and Pete and the change in Jesse's feelings toward his cousin by the end of the story. Remind students to cite textual evidence to support any revisions to their response.

CLOSE READING NOTES

23

Can Animals Feel and Think?

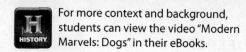

For more context and background, students can view the video "Modern Marvels: Dogs" in their eBooks.

Informational Text by DeShawn Jones

Why This Text

Students may finish reading an informational text without a full understanding of the author's central ideas. Informational texts such as this one by DeShawn Jones may have more than one complex central idea. Remind students that they must identify the central idea when they summarize text. With the help of the close-reading questions, students will determine the central ideas by examining the supporting details. This close reading will lead students to understand the most important ideas and supporting details in an informational text.

Background Have students read the background information about some of the early philosophers and scientists, such as René Descartes, who thought about or studied animal behavior. Introduce the selection by telling students that since the turn of the twenty-first century, many aspects of animal communication, animal emotions, and animal thought processes that experts thought they had understood are being reexamined, and startling new conclusions are being reached.

SETTING A PURPOSE Ask students to pay attention to the central ideas in this informational text and to the author's point of view and purpose for having written this article. How soon into the text can students begin to identify the central idea?

 Common Core Support

- cite textual evidence
- determine a central idea of a text and how it is conveyed through particular details
- provide a summary of a text distinct from personal opinions or judgments
- determine an author's point of view and purpose

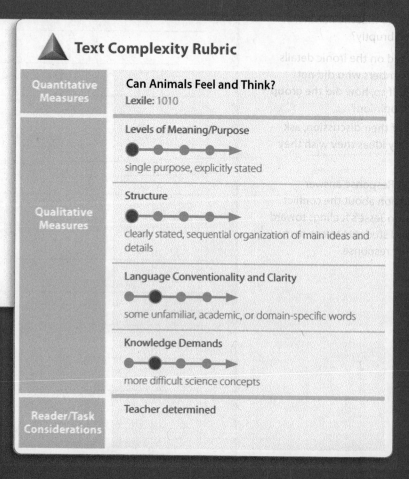

Text Complexity Rubric

Can Animals Feel and Think?
Lexile: 1010

Quantitative Measures

Qualitative Measures

Levels of Meaning/Purpose
single purpose, explicitly stated

Structure
clearly stated, sequential organization of main ideas and details

Language Conventionality and Clarity
some unfamiliar, academic, or domain-specific words

Knowledge Demands
more difficult science concepts

Reader/Task Considerations
Teacher determined

Strategies for CLOSE READING

Summarize Text

Students should read this article carefully all the way through. Close-reading questions at the bottom of the page will help students focus on a central idea and on the details that support it in order to summarize text. As they read, students should record comments or questions about the text in the side margins.

WHEN STUDENTS STRUGGLE . . .

To help students summarize the entire text by focusing on one central idea and its supporting details, have students work in a small group to fill out a chart such as the one shown below as they analyze the informational text.

CITE TEXT EVIDENCE For practice in summarizing, have students first record the central idea and supporting details in the text as a whole or in parts of the text.

Central Idea	Supporting Details
Many scientists now believe that animals, like humans, can feel and think.	Many mammals, such as dogs and elephants, seem to feel emotions such as fear, joy, and grief.
	Some animals, such as pigs and birds, are able to learn or solve problems.
	Animal and human brains have a cerebral cortex, which is responsible for feeling pain, fear, and grief.
	Regardless of brain size, some animals seem to be able to think.
	Animals are more like humans than once thought.

Summary: Scientists now believe that animals, such as mammals and birds, can feel emotions and actually think. Like humans, animals have a cerebral cortex that is responsible for feeling pain, fear, and grief. Also, having a large brain is not necessary for thinking, as evidenced by Betty the crow. Scientists now think that animals are more like humans than once thought.

Background *For most of history, people have believed that animals are totally unlike human beings. A great scholar from the 1600s, René Descartes (dā kärt'), described animals as "machines"—incapable of thinking. In the early 1900s, the scientist Ivan Pavlov performed experiments that led many to believe that animals always acted predictably. In recent years, however, scientists have studied animal emotions and thought processes.*

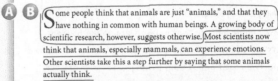

Can Animals Feel and Think?

Informational Text by DeShawn Jones

CLOSE READ Notes

1. **READ ▷** As you read lines 1–13, begin to collect and cite text evidence.

- Circle the central idea in the first paragraph, and underline the details that support the idea.
- Circle the central idea in the second paragraph, and underline the supporting details.
- In the margin, paraphrase each of the two central ideas.

A **B** Some people think that animals are just "animals," and that they have nothing in common with human beings. A growing body of scientific research, however, suggests otherwise. Most scientists now think that animals, especially mammals, can experience emotions. Other scientists take this a step further by saying that some animals actually think.

Think about what most dogs do when you scold them. They lower their heads and slink off to some secluded spot. Only when they sense that you are no longer angry do they come back out. On the other

10 hand, when you return home after a day at school, your dog probably leaps around you, tail wagging furiously. But, do these reactions really indicate that dogs and other mammals feel emotions? They certainly seem to.

Many scientists now believe that animals can feel and think.

Dogs and other mammals seem to feel emotions.

25

---

1. **READ AND CITE TEXT EVIDENCE** Explain that the central idea is the most important idea in the text as a whole or in a paragraph or section of text. Tell students that when you summarize text, you briefly restate in your own words the central idea and the details that support it.

A **ASK STUDENTS** to determine the central idea in each of the first two paragraphs (lines 1–13) and the specific details that convey each central idea. *Responses may include references to the central ideas in lines 1–3 and 11–13 and the supporting details in lines 3–11.*

FOR ELL STUDENTS Explain that "on the other hand" (lines 9–10) is an idiomatic phrase (or expression) that points to a contrast of two things or ideas.

ASK STUDENTS to look for other words and phrases that show comparison, such as *like* or *as*, or contrast, such as *however, while,* and *but,* and cite them in the margin.

C There are plenty of examples that seem to indicate that animals feel emotions such as fear, anger, joy, and grief. If the antelope did not feel fear, it would stand still or continue grazing instead of sprinting away at the sight of a cheetah. Mammals such as dolphins, chimpanzees, and rats show the feeling of joy in their love of playful activity. Elephants show signs of long-lasting grief when a member of
20 the herd dies. Other mammals such as sea lions, bears, and moose also seem to become upset by a death in their group.

Whether or not animals can actually think is a more difficult question. Do animals, for example, have the **capacity** to learn, solve problems, or guess what other animals are thinking? Research suggests that some animals can do this and more.

Chimpanzees in large captive colonies often cooperate with certain other chimpanzees in the colony. They have then been observed to suddenly switch **alliances** and seemingly double-cross each other. This behavior suggests that chimpanzees can, like
30 humans, change their minds or feel **resentment**.

Pigs offer an interesting example of problem solving. A scientist from Bristol University discovered that stronger pigs looking for food would follow the lead of a weaker but smarter pig. The smarter pig would find the food. Then, the smarter pig would trick the stronger pig by distracting it. While the stronger pig wasn't looking, the smarter pig would dive in and gobble up the food.

capacity:
ability

alliances:
loyalties

resentment:
anger

---

2. ◀ REREAD Write a summary of lines 1–13.

Although some people believe that animals are unlike humans, most scientists now think that some animals can feel emotions and actually think. The reactions of dogs when you scold them, for example, seem to confirm that some animals experience emotions.

---

3. READ ▶ As you read lines 14–36, continue to cite textual evidence.

• Circle a sentence in lines 14–21 that informs the reader of the author's point of view.

• Underline at least one fact or example in each paragraph that supports the author's point of view.

The Cerebral Cortex in Different Species

The part of the brain colored pink in these diagrams is the cerebral cortex. The cerebral cortex is the part of the brain that gives the capacity to feel pain, fear, and grief.

D His purpose is to show that animal brains and human brains both have a cerebral cortex.

E Perhaps the most amazing example of an animal thinking involves not a mammal, but a bird. Betty the crow makes her home in a laboratory in Oxford, England. She devised an **ingenious** solution
40 for getting a treat in the form of food that scientists had inserted in a long tube. When she first tried to get the treat, she stuck her beak into the tube but found that the tube was too deep for her beak to reach the treat. Undaunted, she picked up a piece of wire that the scientists had placed beforehand in her cage. She bent the wire into a hook and used the hook to lift the treat from the tube. She did this not once, but repeatedly. What really amazed the scientists observing Betty was that she had never seen a piece of wire before. But this bird figured out the challenge, decided to use the wire, and then shape it into the perfect tool for getting the treat.

ingenious:
clever

---

4. READ ▶ As you read lines 37–53, continue to cite textual evidence.

• Circle the central idea in lines 37–49 and lines 50–53, and underline at least one detail that supports each central idea.

• In the margin, explain the author's purpose for including the diagram, chart, and captions.

---

2. REREAD AND CITE TEXT EVIDENCE

B **ASK STUDENTS** to include each of the two central ideas and supporting details they cited from the first two paragraphs in their summary of lines 1–13. *Responses may include references to lines 1–6 and 7–13.*

3. READ AND CITE TEXT EVIDENCE

C **ASK STUDENTS** to find the author's point of view about the topic and the evidence (details, facts, and examples) he uses to support it. *Students should cite textual evidence from lines 14–36, including references to specific evidence from lines 14–21.*

Critical Vocabulary: capacity (line 23) Have students explain *capacity* as Jones uses it here.

Critical Vocabulary: alliances (line 28) and **resentment** (line 30) Ask students to cite situations in which someone might make alliances with a group but then feel resentment.

4. READ AND CITE TEXT EVIDENCE Explain that the author's purpose is the reason the author writes something. In an informational text, the purpose may be to explain information or even to persuade the reader to agree with the author's point of view.

D **ASK STUDENTS** to read their margin notes to a partner and then explain the author's purpose for including the diagram, labels, and caption, as well as the chart on the next page. *By presenting graphic and textual evidence about animals' brains, Jones is illustrating his point of view about the capacity of some animals to feel and think.*

Critical Vocabulary: ingenious (line 39) Have students explain *ingenious* as Jones uses it here. Why does he use the word to describe Betty the crow? *Jones wants to show that the bird has the ability to problem-solve and even to make a tool, suggesting the capacity of the bird to think.*

The chart and caption demonstrate that brain size does not indicate an animal's intelligence.

Brain Weights of Different Species	
Species	Brain Weight
Elephant	6,000 grams
Adult Human	1,350 grams
Monkey	97 grams
Dog	72 grams
Cat	30 grams
Owl	2.2 grams

Some insects, despite having a brain the size of a pinhead, can seemingly behave as intelligently as bigger animals. Larger animals need larger brains to interpret more sensory information and to control their greater number of muscles.

50 What these examples seem to show is that animals are more like us than we may have once thought. It seems clear that animals can feel a range of emotions. It seems just as clear that some animals show an uncanny ability to do what appears to be "thinking."

5. **◀ REREAD AND DISCUSS** Reread lines 37–53. With a small group, discuss whether the facts and examples the author cites provide sufficient support for his point of view. Be sure to consider the information presented in the diagram, chart, and captions.

SHORT RESPONSE

Cite Text Evidence Write a summary of the article. Review your reading notes, and **cite text evidence** in your summary.

Scientists now think that animals, such as mammals and birds, can feel emotions and actually think. Dogs and elephants appear to show emotions, and chimpanzees and pigs can act in clever, thoughtful ways. A crow shaped a wire into a tool that could help her get food. So, having a large brain is not necessary for thinking. Animals certainly seem capable of thinking and feeling.

28

5. **REREAD AND DISCUSS USING TEXT EVIDENCE** Jones offers graphic and textual evidence to support his point of view.

E **ASK STUDENTS** to appoint a reporter for each group, then cite specific graphic and textual evidence to explain their position as to whether Jones's evidence is sufficient to support his point of view. *Students should cite specific evidence from the diagram and chart, as well as from lines 37–53.*

SHORT RESPONSE

Cite Text Evidence Student responses will vary, but students should use the central idea and supporting details from the text, as well as specific textual evidence, in their summaries. Students should:

- briefly state the central idea of the text as a whole and the details that support it.
- provide a summary distinct from personal opinions or judgments.
- cite specific evidence from the text to support the points made in the summary.

TO CHALLENGE STUDENTS . . .

For more context about animals' abilities and emotions, have students research interesting facts about crows. They can also find videos of Betty the crow online, as well as other videos showing crows using their intelligence in other ways, such as using passing traffic to break nuts.

ASK STUDENTS to share the information they discovered about crows, and how it compares with what they may have previously thought about these birds. *Students may present information about crows being social birds that sometimes live in roosts of hundreds of thousands of individuals. Crows are considered to be among the smartest and most adaptable birds; they can recognize guns and supposedly read traffic lights. They communicate with each other, and there are many tales of their being able to count.*

DIG DEEPER

With the class, return to Question 5, Reread and Discuss. Have students share the results of their discussion.

ASK STUDENTS whether they were pleased with the outcome of their small-group discussions. Have each group share what the majority opinion was regarding the sufficiency of the author's evidence to support his point of view. What convincing evidence did the groups cite from the text to support this opinion?

- Encourage students to tell whether there was any compelling evidence cited by group members holding the opposite opinion. If so, why didn't it sway the group?
- Have groups explain how they decided whether or not they had found sufficient evidence to support their opinion. Did everyone in the group agree as to what made the evidence sufficient? How did the group resolve any conflicts or differences of opinion?

After students have shared the results of their group's discussion, ask whether another group shared any findings they wish they had considered.

ASK STUDENTS to return to their summary of the article in their Short Response answer and to revise it based on the class discussion.

Bats!

Science Writing by Mary Kay Carson

Why This Text

Because science writing often includes not only text but also visual elements, some students may have difficulty integrating the information presented in different formats. The science essay "Bats!" is such a text. With the help of the close-reading questions, students will analyze the text, photographs, illustrations, and charts, using each to enhance their comprehension. This close reading will lead students to develop a deeper understanding of the topic by integrating information presented in different formats.

Background Have students read the background information about bats, the author Mary Kay Carson, and Bat Conservation International (BCI). Introduce the selection by reminding students that in cultures worldwide, people may tell scary stories or anecdotes about bats, such as that bats are the souls of sleeping people or that bats in a building means something evil will happen. Encourage students to share their own stories. Then, tell students that this article will give them real facts about what it turns out are pretty amazing creatures.

SETTING A PURPOSE Ask students to pay attention to the information given in the text and the information presented in photographs, illustrations, and charts. Tell them to note how visual elements add to their understanding of the text.

 Common Core Support

- cite textual evidence
- analyze how a key idea is introduced, illustrated, and elaborated in a text
- integrate information presented in different formats

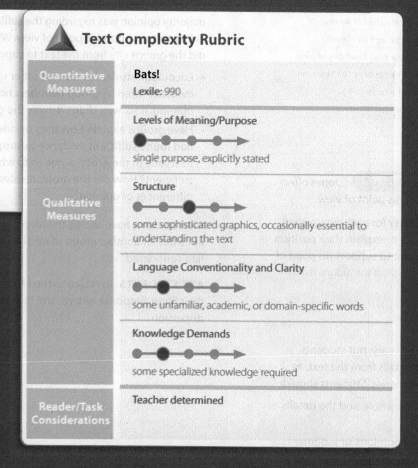

Text Complexity Rubric

Quantitative Measures

Bats!
Lexile: 990

Qualitative Measures

Levels of Meaning/Purpose

single purpose, explicitly stated

Structure

some sophisticated graphics, occasionally essential to understanding the text

Language Conventionality and Clarity

some unfamiliar, academic, or domain-specific words

Knowledge Demands

some specialized knowledge required

Reader/Task Considerations

Teacher determined

Integrate Information

Students should read this science essay carefully all the way through. Close-reading questions at the bottom of the page will help them to collect and cite text evidence to better understand the text. As they read, students should jot down comments or questions about the text in the margins.

WHEN STUDENTS STRUGGLE . . .

To help students integrate information in "Bats!," have them work in small groups to fill out a chart like the one shown below.

CITE TEXT EVIDENCE For practice in integrating information, ask students to tell what text evidence supports the facts given by the author.

Text Feature	Information It Provides
Selection Text (pages 29–34)	The text explains what makes bats such unique creatures.
A Bat's Body (page 30)	The illustrations and labels help convey what happens when bats fly and what happens if these parts are injured.
Echolocation: Seeing with Sound (page 33)	The graphic and text explains and clarifies the process of echolocation.
Batty Myths (page 34)	This feature gives examples of popular misconceptions about bats.

Background *Austin, Texas is home to millions of bats. It's also home to Bat Conservation International (BCI), an organization that works to conserve the world's bats and the environments where they live. In this excerpt from* The Bat Scientist, *nature writer Mary Kay Carson introduces Barbara French, a bat biologist who worked as science officer at BCI for 15 years. She now rescues and rehabilitates bats in Texas.*

Bats!

Science Writing by Mary Kay Carson

CLOSE READ
Notes

1. **READ ▷** As you read lines 1–29, begin to collect and cite text evidence.
   • Circle facts about bats that make them different from humans.
   • Make notes in the margin about what happens to the bats after they have recovered in Barbara's care.

Barbara cares for a half-dozen or so different kinds of bats, including orphaned red bat babies, injured Mexican free-tailed bats, **recuperating** evening bats and yellow bats, captive straw-colored fruit bats, and an elderly cave bat. They're representatives of just a few of the world's thousand-plus bat species. Bats live on every continent

A except Antarctica. They come in all sizes—from as small as a hummingbird to as big as an owl. More than one-fifth of all five thousand or so mammal species are bats.

Flight is what makes bats unique. They became the only truly
10 flying mammal more than 50 million years ago. The secret is their wings. Bat wings are made of naked skin over a framework of bones—the same bones we have. Barbara gently unfolds the wing of a Mexican free-tailed bat. "There's her elbow and her wrist," says Barbara as she touches the bones visible through the wing's thin skin.

recuperating:
recovering;
improving

29

---

1. **READ AND CITE TEXT EVIDENCE** The author tells readers that bats come in all sizes.

   A **ASK STUDENTS** to find the examples cited by the author to prove that bats come in all sizes. *Bats can be as small as a hummingbird or as big as an owl.*

   Critical Vocabulary: recuperating (line 3) Have students share their definitions of *recuperating*. Ask why a recuperating bat might need the kind of help Barbara offers them. *Because the bats are recovering from some sort of injury, Barbara can help them get well faster and also determine when they are well enough to be set free.*

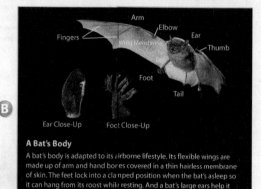

Arm
Elbow
Ear
Fingers
Thumb
Wing Membrane
Foot
Tail

B

Ear Close-Up   Foot Close-Up

A Bat's Body

A bat's body is adapted to its airborne lifestyle. Its flexible wings are made up of arm and hand bones covered in a thin hairless membrane of skin. The feet lock into a clamped position when the bat's asleep so it can hang from its roost while resting. And a bat's large ears help it hear the echoed sounds it bounces off prey and obstacles in flight.

maneuver:

to change movement or direction

Barbara releases the bats that are able to fly and feed themselves. The bats that can't fly or find food travel with Barbara as bat ambassadors.

"And her thumb," she continues, pointing to the small nub[1] halfway down the top of the wing. Bats are master fliers. Their flapping wings propel them forward with speed and **maneuver** them around trees, after insects, and into crevices.[2]

When a bat can't fly, it's in trouble. Many of Barbara's bat patients
20 have broken or hurt wings. "The wing injuries can often be treated," says Barbara. She sometimes does bat surgery, putting pins in the broken bones. "Finger injuries will heal well, but the upper arm is much harder," says Barbara. Only bats that can fly and catch insects on their own are released back into the wild. Outside the bat barn is a big flight cage where recuperating bats exercise and can catch bugs. When—and if—they can feed themselves, Barbara releases them back into the wild. Those that can't make it on their own become bat ambassadors, traveling with Barbara to events that teach people the truth about bats.

30 Bats are unique among mammals in other ways besides flight. In general, the bigger the mammal, the longer it lives. An elephant might live seventy years, a dog fifteen years, or a hamster only two years.

[1] **nub:** bump, bony protrusion.
[2] **crevices:** small gaps.

30

Bats break this rule. Even small bats can live forty or more years. For their size, bats are the longest-lived mammals on earth. Bats also reproduce slowly for their size. A mouse might have dozens of babies per year. Most kinds of bats give birth only once a year to a single pup. "One lost bat baby is a lost generation," says Barbara.

While the bat babies get milk, most adults in the bat barn eat live
C
mealworms. "They're live beetle **larvae**," says Barbara. "I order eighty
40 thousand mealworms a month." Most North American bats are insect-eaters. They have mouths full of sharp teeth to quickly crunch up insects as they fly. Each of the 1,100 different kinds of bats is especially adapted to the particular food it eats. Fruit-eating bats have big eyes and powerful noses to see and smell the ripe tropical fruit available year round. Nectar-eating bats also live in warm places with year-round flowers. They have long noses and tongues to reach deep into flowers and slurp up nectar. There are bats that snag fish with their strong-clawed feet, bats that catch birds in midair, and even bats that ambush mice on the ground! The infamous vampire bats of
50 Central and South America drink the blood of mammals and birds.
D
Most bats do their eating at night. They are nocturnal animals. So how do bats manage to fly around and find their food in the dark? Many fruit-eating bats have extra-big eyes, just like other nocturnal creatures. The African straw-colored fruit bats that Barbara cares for have dog-like faces—the reason these kinds of bats are often called flying foxes. "They depend on their eyesight and sense of smell to find fruit," explains Barbara.

larvae:

young, wingless, often wormlike form of an insect

2. **REREAD** Reread lines 9–18. Underline the parts of a bat's body that humans also have. Study the image of the bat. How does showing body parts similar to a human's help you better understand a bat's body? Support your answer with explicit textual evidence.

A bat's body is like a human's because they both have common parts: arms, fingers, and ears. But humans do not have wings or large ears that help them find food.

3. **READ** As you read lines 30–85, continue to cite textual evidence.

• Underline text that explains how bats get food, including their use of sound.
• Make brief notes about echolocation in the margin.

31

Critical Vocabulary: maneuver (line 17) The text says that *maneuvering* is something that helps bats get around trees, find insects, and get into small places. Have students share examples of when they had to maneuver in order to do something or get someplace. Then, ask students to share their definitions of *maneuver*.

FOR ELL STUDENTS Clarify the meaning of *ambassadors* in this context. Explain that in politics, an ambassador is the representative of a country's government in another country. In this text, the bats that can't fly "represent" all the other bats in Barbara's events and lectures.

2. **REREAD AND CITE TEXT EVIDENCE**

B **ASK STUDENTS** to explain how the information in the graphic helps them understand the information in lines 13–24. *Seeing the bat's fingers, arm, elbow, and other parts helps me to understand how it flies and what happens when these parts are injured.*

3. **READ AND CITE TEXT EVIDENCE**

C **ASK STUDENTS** to cite text evidence in lines 39–50 that shows how different bats have adapted to eat different foods. *North American bats have sharp teeth to crunch insects as they fly; fruit-eating bats have big eyes and powerful noses to see and smell fruit; nectar-eating bats have long noses and tongues to reach deep into flowers; some bats snag fish with their strong-clawed feet.*

Critical Vocabulary: larvae (line 39) Barbara orders eighty thousand beetle larvae a month for the bats to eat. Ask students what, based on this fact, they think the larvae will look like. Then, ask students to share their definitions of *larvae*.

Insect-eating bats are different. "Hearing is most important for them," says Barbara. "They can also smell and see, but echolocation is
60 the biggest part of finding their food." These bats get around and hunt in the dark by "seeing" with sound.

E Echolocation means locating something with echoes. Like sonar, it's a way to get information about something by bouncing sounds off it. Echolocating bats make loud calls and then listen for the echoes. The reflected sounds carry information about distance, speed, density, and size. A bat's brain turns the information into a kind of picture that helps the night-flying bat avoid trees, zero in on prey, and speed through caves. An echolocating bat "sees" its surroundings—caves, telephone poles, other bats, birds, and its prey—with sound. Bat
70 echolocation is so precise that a bat can find a moth, tell how big it is, and know in which direction and at what speed it's moving, all in complete darkness. And it gathers all this information quickly enough to catch the moth while flying through a forest.

"It's why echolocators have such large ears," explains Barbara. Their big, sensitive ears collect the echoes like tiny satellite dishes. The strange faces of many bats are also echolocation tools. Those wrinkly lips and ears, leaf-shaped snouts called noseleafs, and bumpy foreheads focus the calls and echoes. Some bats even shout their calls through their megaphone-like nose. Bats are the loudest flying
80 animals around! Their short calls or shouts are as loud as a smoke detector. Luckily for us, those echolocation calls are ultrasonic—too high pitched for humans to hear. So what is all the plainly heard chatter about inside Barbara's bat barn? "They're communicating," explains Barbara. Besides using ultrasonic calls to echolocate, bats use **audible** chirps, trills, buzzes, clicks, and purrs to talk to one another.

Echolocation lets bats "see" things by bouncing sounds off what is in front of them. This is how they catch food.

audible:
clear, loud

---

4. ◀ REREAD AND DISCUSS Reread lines 51–61. In a small group, discuss the following question: If bats can see quite well, why is echolocation important to them?

5. READ ▶ As you read lines 86–107 and the list of "Batty Myths" on page 34, continue to cite evidence.

• Underline ways that bats communicate with one another.
• Circle two ways that bats are important to their ecosystems.
• Underline three "batty" myths that you find surprising.

32

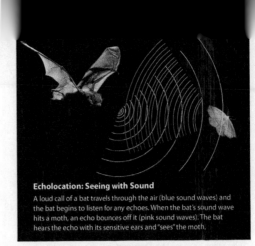

Echolocation: Seeing with Sound
A loud call of a bat travels through the air (blue sound waves) and the bat begins to listen for any echoes. When the bat's sound wave hits a moth, an echo bounces off it (pink sound waves). The bat hears the echo with its sensitive ears and "sees" the moth.

F What do bats talk about? The normal stuff—food, friends, mates, territory, and complaints. The most talkative bats seem to be those that live in big colonies. Think of the mother bat coming home to Bracken Bat Cave after a night of hunting bugs. How does she find her
90 pup among the millions of bats? One way she zeros in on her baby is by calling to it, and then the pup calls back to her. Barbara and other scientists have identified more than twenty different calls in Mexican free-tailed bats. Many were first discovered from studying the recorded conversations among the colony of fifty or so free-tailed bats in Barbara's barn. "They may even use a sort of grammar," says Barbara. "They put all of these little clicks and buzzes and trills together in certain ways to make certain meanings."

The fact that bats communicate with a complex language adds to what scientists are learning about these marvelous and misunderstood
100 mammals. Though many people once scorned them as flying **vermin**, we now know that bats are intelligent, social, long-lived creatures more closely related to monkeys than mice. And no matter where they live or what they eat, each bat species plays an important role in its ecosystem. Bats are important controllers of insects. Fruit bats pollinate plants and spread seeds that grow forests. Cave-dwelling bats and the guano[3] they make support hundreds of unique cave species of insects, fungi,[4] and bacteria found nowhere else.

---
[3] **guano:** the waste that bats produce.
[4] **fungi:** mushrooms.

vermin:
pests

33

---

4. REREAD AND DISCUSS USING TEXT EVIDENCE

D **ASK STUDENTS** to assign a reporter for each group to present specific text evidence to support what they have learned about bats. Building on their text evidence, have students discuss how bats differ from other mammals, why flying is so important to bats, and what the eating habits of bats are.

5. READ AND CITE TEXT EVIDENCE

E **ASK STUDENTS** Ask students to find and cite information both in the text and in the illustration caption on p. 33 that explains how bats hear and the importance of echolocation. *Students should cite information in lines 62–73 as well as information from the illustration and the caption.*

Critical Vocabulary: audible (line 85) The text gives examples of things that are audible, such as chirps, trills, buzzes, clicks, and purrs. Based on this, what do you think the word *audible* means?

Critical Vocabulary: vermin (line 100) Have students share their definitions of *vermin*. Ask them why the appearance of vermin at a family picnic would be a disaster. *The presence of vermin would disgust people and ruin the picnic.*

BATTY MYTHS

People still believe all kinds of crazy things about bats. Here are six of the most commonly misunderstood bat facts.

Bats Are Not Blind. All bats have eyes and can see quite well.

Most Bats Do Not Have Rabies. Like any wild animal, bats should not be touched, especially one found on the ground, which is more likely to be sick. However, getting rabies from a bat is very rare.

Bats Do Not Get Tangled In People's Hair. Bats are too good at flying for that— plus they generally avoid humans.

Bats Do Not Suck Blood. Not even the three species of vampire bats that live in Central and South America suck blood. They lap it up with their tiny tongues. No vampire bats live in the United States, except in zoos.

Bats Are Not Flying Mice. DNA evidence shows that bats are not closely related to rodents. Some scientists believe they are more like **primitive** primates.

Bats Are Not Pests In Need Of Extermination. Bats can be safely removed from an attic or home without harming them. Bats are important pest controllers, often eating their own weight in pest insects every night.

primitive:
simple, not advanced

6. **◀ REREAD** Reread lines 86–97. Why might bats in big colonies be the most talkative?

Bats in big colonies might be most talkative because they have to communicate with many other bats.

SHORT RESPONSE

Cite Text Evidence Explain how the information in the photos helps you understand the ways insect-eating bats communicate and find food. Be sure to **cite text evidence** in your response.

The picture of the bat and the moth shows the bat using echolocation, which lets the bat "see" its food. Both pictures show the bat's ears, which let it hear the echo of whatever is in front of it. The bat then knows how big something is and how quickly it's moving. The echolocation calls that bats use to find prey are ultrasonic, but they use other sounds to communicate with each other. They use sounds like buzzes and clicks to make a complex language.

34

TO CHALLENGE STUDENTS . . .

For more context about bats and organizations devoted to their protection, students can research the Ann W. Richards Congress Avenue Bridge in Austin, Texas, and the work done by Bat Conservation International (BTI) to both educate people about bats and protect bats and their habitats.

ASK STUDENTS what they have learned about the bats that spend their summers in Austin, Texas, at the Ann W. Richards Congress Avenue Bridge. Why do the bats go there? *They migrate from Mexico and stay under the bridge because it is safe and protected.* What kinds of bats are attracted to the area? *For the most part, the area is populated by Mexican free-tailed bats.* Why does the presence of bats attract tourists? *Tourists are attracted to the area because of the huge number of bats there in the summer—about 1.5 million (more than the population of Austin).* What contributions has Bat Conservation International (BTI) made to protect bats in the area? *BTI has educated the population about bats, telling residents that they have nothing to fear as long as they don't try to handle the bats. As a result, residents have grown to appreciate the bats and their contribution to the city.* What other work does BTI do? *BTI works worldwide to protect bats from persecution by humans, habitat loss, and environmental pollution.*

---

6. **REREAD AND CITE TEXT EVIDENCE**

F **ASK STUDENTS** to provide reasons to support their ideas on why bats in large colonies would be more talkative. *Students should mention that bats in large colonies have more bats to communicate with and may learn many different calls.*

Critical Vocabulary: primitive (line 13 in the list of Batty Myths) Have students share their definitions of *primitive*. What does the phrase *primitive primate* mean? *an early form of primate, a primate in an early stage of development*

SHORT RESPONSE

Cite Text Evidence Students' responses will vary but should include evidence from photos and illustrations that support their answers. Students should:

- explain how bats communicate.
- explain how bats find food.

DIG DEEPER

With the class, return to Question 4, Reread. Have students share the results of their discussion.

ASK STUDENTS what additional information they have learned about bats, in particular how they hear and what they contribute to ecosystems. Remind students to cite text and visual evidence that supports what they have learned.

- Have students explain echolocation and why it is a unique ability. *Echolocation allows bats to get information about something by bouncing sounds off of it. As they use echolocation, bats make loud sounds and then listen for the echoes. The reflected sound of the echoes carries information about distance, speed, density, and size. This information enables the bat to "see" its surroundings.*

- Encourage students to use information gleaned from the chart and illustration on page 33. *The illustration in the chart shows how a bat tracks the sound made by a moth. The sound waves made by the moth travel and send a message (an echo) back to the bats. This echo allows bats, with their highly sensitive ears, to "see" the moth.*

- Have groups summarize their findings on bats and discuss why or why not bats are good for ecosystems. *Flight is what makes bats unique because they are the only mammal that can fly. When a bat can't fly, it's in trouble because without flying it has no way to get food. Bats feed mostly on insects, but different kinds of bats have developed different methods for catching and eating their food. Bats are nocturnal animals, which means that they are active only at night. But, because of echolocation they can "see" and hunt at night. Their heightened sense of smell also helps bats hunt at night. Bats make all kinds of sounds and appear to be able to communicate with each other in a complex language, especially when they are gathered together in large colonies. Bats are important controllers of insects and wherever they are they play an important role in their ecosystem. Most of the myths about bats—for example, that they are blind or get tangled in people's hair—are not true.*

ASK STUDENTS to return their Short Responses and revise them based on their discussion.

CLOSE READING NOTES

Dealing with Disaster

Dealing with Disaster

"Through every kind of disaster and setback and catastrophe. We are survivors."

—Robert Fulghum

BOOK REVIEW

Moby-Duck

David Holahan

SHORT STORY

There Will Come Soft Rains

Ray Bradbury

NEWSPAPER ARTICLE

On the Titanic, Defined by What They Wore

Guy Trebay

Moby-Duck

Book Review by David Holahan

Why This Text

Students may have difficulty reading book reviews because not only must they follow the reviewer's analysis of the book, but they must also assess the review itself. With the help of the close-reading questions, students will analyze how cause-and-effect relationships—along with information presented in a map—help the reviewer organize his thoughts about the book. This close reading will lead students to understand the review and the book.

Background Have students read the background and information about the lost cargo of bath toys. The problem of ocean pollution has gained the attention of the media and public in recent years. Most of the articles produced and consumed today—from food containers to cell phones to cars—are made with plastic or plastic components. A great deal of this plastic does not end up in landfills. Rather, it finds its way into rivers, which lead almost invariably to the ocean.

SETTING A PURPOSE Ask students to pay attention to how cause-and-effect relationships underlie much of the book review. How does the reviewer use them to organize his writing?

Common Core Support

- cite textual evidence
- determine a central idea of a text
- determine the meaning of words
- analyze how particular elements of a text fit into its structure
- determine an author's point of view
- integrate information presented in different formats

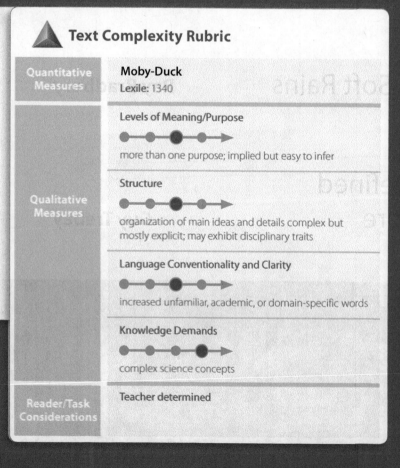

Text Complexity Rubric

Quantitative Measures	**Moby-Duck** Lexile: 1340
Qualitative Measures	**Levels of Meaning/Purpose** — more than one purpose; implied but easy to infer
	Structure — organization of main ideas and details complex but mostly explicit; may exhibit disciplinary traits
	Language Conventionality and Clarity — increased unfamiliar, academic, or domain-specific words
	Knowledge Demands — complex science concepts
Reader/Task Considerations	Teacher determined

Analyze Structure

Students should read this book review carefully all the way through. Close-reading questions at the bottom of the page will help them focus on a thorough analysis of the cause-and-effect relationships. As they read, students should jot down comments or questions about the text in the margins.

WHEN STUDENTS STRUGGLE . . .

To help students analyze the structure of Holahan's review, have them work in small groups to fill out a chart like the one shown below.

CITE TEXT EVIDENCE For practice in analyzing the structure of a book review, ask students to cite text evidence for some of the cause-and-effect relationships.

Cause	Effect(s)
28,800 plastic ducks spill into the north Pacific.	". . . the author's quest more than a decade later to track their journey . . ." (lines 12–13)
Donovan Hohn decides to write a book about the lost plastic ducks.	"He would . . . help to clean up beaches in Alaska . . ." (lines 23–24) "The author also trolled for plastic on the high seas . . ." (lines 27–28)
Ocean currents in the north Pacific are circular.	"Two thousand of the Floatees . . . are stuck in . . . the North Pacific Gyre." (caption, p. 39) ". . . where our floating industrial waste stream often is aggregated." (lines 34–35)
Plastic things are meant to be thrown away.	". . . barely five percent of all plastic we use is recycled." (lines 59–60) ". . . that's what makes them so . . . profitable" (lines 61–62)

Background *In 1992, a cargo ship departed from Hong Kong for Tacoma, Washington. During a storm, thousands of plastic bath toys called Friendly Floatees were washed overboard. Oceanographers later used these toys to study ocean currents. Some Floatees reached distant British shores more than ten years after the storm.*

Moby-Duck

Book Review by David Holahan

CLOSE READ
Notes

1. **READ ▶** As you read lines 1–31, begin to collect and cite evidence.
   • Underline what will happen to readers who read *Moby-Duck*.
   • In the margin, explain what the book's subtitle lets you know.
   • In the margin, summarize lines 19–31.

Donovan Hohn's narrative about his monomaniacal[1] quest for the elusive yellow duck(s) bobbing somewhere upon the **intractable** oceans is more than a little Melvillian.[2] The plastic (not rubber) duckies that were cast so carelessly upon the waters are a symbol of our collective, all-consuming sin. Readers of this book will never again smile benignly at cloying little bath toys.

The plot of *Moby-Duck* (which has an epically long subtitle: "The True Story of 28,800 Bath Toys Lost at Sea and of the Beachcombers, Oceanographers, Environmentalists, and Fools, Including the Author,

10 Who Went In Search of Them") revolves around the 1992 spill of 28,800 bathtub accessories from a massive container ship in the north Pacific, and the author's quest more than a decade later to track their

---

[1] **monomaniacal:** obsessed with one idea or subject.
[2] **Melvillian:** similar to the writings of author Herman Melville, specifically to the novel *Moby Dick*, the tale of a crew in search of a great white whale.

intractable:
uncontrollable

The book is about the author's quest to learn more about thousands of bath toys lost at sea.

37

1. **READ AND CITE TEXT EVIDENCE** Explain to students that the book's title, *Moby-Duck*, is a play on words referring to the great nineteenth-century whaling novel, *Moby Dick*.

A **ASK STUDENTS** why Holahan might open his review by telling readers that the book will change their view about plastic bath toys. *Students should recognize that the reviewer thinks the book is a success. Before reading the book, a person might see "cloying little bath toys." But after reading it, the person will see "a symbol of our collective, all-consuming sin." Reading the book, then, will cause people to learn important lessons about seemingly mundane items.*

Critical Vocabulary: intractable (line 2) Have students share their definitions of *intractable*. What makes the oceans intractable? *They are huge. They are deep and cover the planet. The currents and waves are strong and never stop.*

Hohn was going to write about the spill from home, but got actively involved in tracking plastic flotsam around the world.

disgorged:
poured out

charismatic:
appealing; charming

journey from China to purportedly pristine places like Hawaii and Alaska, and possibly through Northwest Passage to Maine. Will the author find one of these indestructible icons of domestic bliss on the bounding main, or along some secluded spit of sand, as other beachcombers have? Or will his odyssey end in failure, like that of the doomed Pequod?[3]

B 20   A former school teacher, Hohn got the idea for the book from a student's essay about the spill and toyed with the idea of writing about it from the safety of his home in New York City. His wife was expecting, after all. But he soon was consumed by the watery tale and the search for answers. So off he went, again and again. He would comb and help to clean up beaches in Alaska, which—despite being America's "Last Frontier"—is awash in startling amounts of debris: fishing gear, bottles, cans and the rest of the relentless plastic flotsam of our ever expanding civilization. The author also trolled for plastic on the high seas, shoved off with scientists studying oceanic currents,

30   and booked a cruise on a container ship like the one that **disgorged** all those duckies (beavers, frogs, and turtles spilled, too, but these, clearly, are less **charismatic** commercial litter).

[3] **Pequod:** Captain Ahab's ship in Melville's novel *Moby Dick*.

---

2. ◀ REREAD Reread lines 19–31. Look up and define the words *debris* and *flotsam*. Use these words to explain where Hohn's search led him and what he found.

"Debris" means scattered remains or rubble. "Flotsam" means wreckage that floats after a ship has sunk. Hohn's search led him to beaches in Alaska, where he cleaned up vast amounts of debris, including bottles and cans. He also looked for flotsam in the high seas, studied oceanic currents, and rode on a container ship.

3. READ ▶ As you read lines 32–41, continue to cite text evidence.
   - Underline what people once believed about the ocean.
   - Study the map showing where ocean currents carried the shipwrecked toys.
   - Underline information about the Great Pacific Garbage Patch in the text and in the caption.

North Pacific Gyre
1995   Nov.1992   2003
Tacoma 1996   2007
Hong Kong   Jan.1992   2000/2003

C This map shows where the Floatees traveled between the time they went overboard in 1992 and 2007. Two thousand of the Floatees, along with the Great Pacific Garbage Patch, are stuck in the circular currents of the North Pacific Gyre.

D   Cleaning up a remote beach where grizzly bears forage is hardly the answer to plastic pollution, it turns out. The shoreline will be well littered again in no time. And where does that leave the oceans, where our floating industrial waste stream often is aggregated by the currents into places with names like the Great Pacific Garbage Patch? The oceans were once thought to be too vast for us to properly befoul—even Rachel Carson[4] thought as much for a time. The Great Pacific Garbage Patch is roughly the size of Texas and growing, and

40   plastic has become as common as plankton in many places. Birds and fish mistake the smaller portions for food.

[4] **Rachel Carson:** American conservationist, scientist, ecologist, and marine biologist; often credited with being the founder of the environmental movement.

---

4. ◀ REREAD AND DISCUSS Review lines 32–41 and the map. With a small group, integrate information from the text and the map to explain the many effects of a single cause: the spill of 28,800 bathtub toys.

5. READ ▶ As you read lines 42–54, continue to cite text evidence. Underline the descriptive words and phrases Holahan uses to describe Hohn's writing.

---

2. **REREAD AND CITE TEXT EVIDENCE**

B ASK STUDENTS what caused Hohn to search for the toy ducks. *He read a student essay about the toy duck spill and was consumed by the story. He wanted to get answers.*

3. **READ AND CITE TEXT EVIDENCE**

C ASK STUDENTS to discuss the effects of ocean currents on plastic trash. *The map shows that the currents move plastic trash all over the world. But some of the currents are circular, so they aggregate the trash in giant "garbage patches."*

Critical Vocabulary: disgorged (line 29) Have students give the meaning of the base word *gorged. ate greedily* So what does *disgorged* mean? *threw out*

Critical Vocabulary: charismatic (line 31) Have students suggest synonyms of the adjective *charismatic. appealing, alluring, charming, magnetic*

4. **REREAD AND DISCUSS USING TEXT EVIDENCE**

D ASK STUDENTS in each group to describe three chains of events: one that leads to the author on an Alaskan beach, one that leads to 2,000 Floatees in the Great Pacific Garbage Patch, and one that leads to birds and fish eating plastic. *Students may want to draw a flowchart to show these cause-and-effect chains. They should note the following chains: 1) Toys spill ➔ student essay ➔ Hohn consumed by story ➔ Hohn travels to Alaska; 2) Toys spill ➔ currents move toys ➔ 2,000 toys stuck in North Pacific Gyre; 3) toys spill ➔ currents move toys and other plastic trash ➔ birds and fish eat small pieces of plastic.*

5. **READ AND CITE TEXT EVIDENCE**

E ASK STUDENTS to summarize what Holahan says about Hohn's writing. *Students should explain that Holahan thinks Hohn is an accomplished writer whose style suits his subject.*

E
F
Hohn, who is now the features editor at *GQ* [magazine], writes with precision and passion about what he sees and learns on his various travels and about his discussions with scientists, mariners, do-gooders, and beachcombers. His writing is lively and literate, filled with vivid descriptions, telling context, and lightly seasoned with quotes from Melville and others. He knows a symbol when one bobs into his **ken**, and what to do with it: "Here, then, is one of the
50 meanings of the duck. It represents this vision of childhood—the hygienic childhood, the safe childhood, the brightly colored childhood in which everything, even bathtub articles, have been designed to please the childish mind, much as the golden fruit in that most famous origin myth of paradise 'was pleasant to the eyes' of childish Eve."

ken:
knowledge;
awareness

6. **‹ REREAD** Reread lines 42–54. Is this a positive or negative review of Hohn's book? Cite evidence from the text to support your answer.

This is a positive review of Hohn's book. Holahan praises Hohn by saying he writes with "precision and passion." He compliments his writing by calling it "lively and literate" and says that Hohn uses "vivid descriptions." Holahan also provides a quotation from the book to give an example of Hohn's effective use of symbols.

7. **READ ›** As you read lines 55–78, continue to cite text evidence.

- Circle environmental "cons" and underline real solutions to reducing the amount of trash in the ocean.
- Explain in the margin what the technique of "greenwashing" means. Be sure to read the footnote that defines the term.

40

"So what is the answer to oceans beset by a rising tide of indestructible trash?"

H
G
The author also knows a clever con when he sees one. He concludes that "Keep America Beautiful" approaches, which are largely spawned and bankrolled by the very corporations that are producing all the plastic detritus, are not the answer. There is no way to keep much of anything beautiful when barely five percent of all
60 plastic we use is recycled. The whole point of plastic things is that they are made to be thrown away; that's what makes them so darn consumer-friendly and profitable. What companies are doing with their "Let's Not Litter" PR is to "greenwash"[5] their own sizeable and systemic culpability, according to Hohn.
So what is the answer to oceans beset by a rising tide of indestructible trash? One is people like boat captain Charlie Moore, a self-made scientist and activist, who works to raise public awareness of the problem and lobbies for more enlightened regulations and corporate practices. Others Hohn encounters are volunteering their
70 time and money to clean up our collective mess.

Greenwashing is a technique companies use to appear concerned about the environment when they may actually be doing the environment harm.

[5] **greenwashing:** a practice in which a company deceptively promotes the idea that its product is good for the environment when that is not the case.

41

---

6. **REREAD AND CITE TEXT EVIDENCE**

F **ASK STUDENTS** to cite phrases with positive connotations that tell them that the reviewer admires Hohn's work. *Students should cite phrases that are complimentary of Hohn's writing ability.*

7. **READ AND CITE TEXT EVIDENCE** Holahan introduces the term "greenwash" to describe corporations' attempts to appear environmentally friendly. The term is an adaptation of the verb *whitewash*—to cover up one's crimes or sins.

G **ASK STUDENTS** what might cause a company to pursue a *greenwashing* campaign. *Students should note that the companies "are producing all the plastic detritus." They need customers to keep buying their products, so they want customers to have favorable ideas about the companies and their products.*

Critical Vocabulary: ken (line 48) Have students share their definitions of *ken*, and ask them to use the noun in sentences.

FOR ELL STUDENTS Point out the phrase *a clever con* in line 55. Tell students that the term means "a swindle" or "a trick." The word *con* is an abbreviation for *confidence,* and the kind of swindle it describes involves first winning the victim's confidence.

But the author wonders if such solutions, nibbling around the edges, are enough: "I'd like to share Moore's faith in the arc of progress . . . but I had a hard time imagining the bright future he saw, in which we Americans would trade conspicuous consumption for cradle-to-cradle manufacturing practices, disposable plastics for zero-waste policies and closed ecological loops. I had a hard time because such a future seemed to me **inimical** to the American gospel of perpetual economic growth."

inimical:
unfriendly; hostile

8. ◄ **REREAD** Reread lines 55–78. Summarize why certain actions are "cons," according to Hohn.

Certain companies that make plastic products will fund campaigns about keeping the environment clean but do not change their practices. Hohn calls these actions "cons" because they are deceptive.

SHORT RESPONSE

Cite Text Evidence At the beginning of this review, Holahan says that "Readers of this book will never again smile" at "little bath toys." Do you agree or disagree with this statement, now that you know about the life of the Floatees? Support your response by **citing text evidence**.

Sample response: I agree with Holahan's statement about the Floatees. Before reading this review, I never imagined that these little yellow ducks could be a part of a "floating industrial waste stream." But now that I have learned about the spill described in the book and how far the ducks spread from the map, I will view the "little bath toys" differently from now on. They symbolize a huge environmental problem that impacts people all over the world.

42

8. **REREAD AND CITE TEXT EVIDENCE**

Ⓗ **ASK STUDENTS** to discuss the results of the cons mentioned by the reviewer. *The cons can lead to consumers being fooled: buying and throwing away plastic products while they believe that recycling "keeps America beautiful." Consumers will think favorably of companies with a "let's not litter" message, even though those very companies are to blame for plastic trash.*

Critical Vocabulary: inimical (line 77) Have students suggest synonyms of *inimical* that could be used in this context. *opposed, adverse, unfavorable*

SHORT RESPONSE

Cite Text Evidence Students should:

- tell whether they agree or disagree with the statement.
- explain how they viewed bath toys before reading the essay.
- give examples of the effect of the essay on their opinions.

40

TO CHALLENGE STUDENTS . . .

To deepen their knowledge of the problem of ocean plastics, students can research the causes and effects online.

ASK STUDENTS to research where most of the plastic trash in oceans comes from. Students can pursue this topic by investigating the paths that plastic takes to reach oceans, or by examining what kinds of plastic objects are found in oceans. *Students should realize that most plastic trash is consumer waste that washes into gutters, streams, and rivers that flow into the ocean. Coastal towns and cities are the main source of this kind of plastic. Fishing boats are another major source. The global fishing fleet is enormous—and responsible for a staggering amount of flotsam such as abandoned nets. The shipping industry, from container ships to cruise liners, is the last major source. Anything that washes off these boats—bags, Styrofoam, nylon ropes, plastic ducks—becomes ocean trash.*

Have students research some of the consequences of plastic trash in the oceans. This topic relates mainly to marine animals and ocean ecosystems. *Students should note that ocean plastic gradually breaks down into smaller and smaller pieces. The tiniest pieces are taken up by microorganisms, thus entering the food chain. Larger pieces are eaten directly by fish, seabirds, and turtles. And the largest pieces—nets, lines, and ropes—pose deadly hazards to some of the ocean's most charismatic animals, such as dolphins, seals, otters, and whales.*

DIG DEEPER

1. With the class, return to Question 1, Read. Have students share their explanations of the book's subtitle.

   ASK STUDENTS to discuss how Holahan uses the subtitle as a device to help frame his review.

   - Have students reread lines 7–31 and cite text evidence of the groups mentioned in the subtitle. Students should realize that Holahan gives an overview of the book by telling how the author, at various points in his quest, joins each of the groups that are searching for the plastic ducks. *Holahan writes that the author wonders whether he will find a duck on "some secluded spit of sand, as other beachcombers have" (lines 16–17). He writes that the author will later "comb and help to clean up beaches in Alaska" (line 24), thus joining the ranks of beachcombers and environmentalists. And finally Holahan notes that the author sails with "scientists studying oceanic currents" (line 28)— that is, oceanographers.*

2. With the class, return to Question 4, Reread and Discuss. Have students share the main points of their discussion.

   ASK STUDENTS why cleaning up the plastic on beaches is not a solution to plastic pollution.

   - Students should understand that cleaning up beaches only addresses a result of the problem, not the cause. *The sources of plastic pollution aren't changed by cleaning up beaches. Plastic trash will still get into the ocean, and ocean currents will still move it onto beaches. Until people stop letting trash get into the oceans, the beaches will be littered with plastic.*

   ASK STUDENTS to return to their Short Response answer and revise it based on the class discussion.

CLOSE READING NOTES

There Will Come Soft Rains

Short Story by Ray Bradbury

Why This Text

Students may have difficulty accepting the idea of a story where the main character is a house with human attributes. In "There Will Come Soft Rains," Ray Bradbury uses a "dying" house to represent his vision of the future—a post-apocalyptic world devoid of humans, one in which a house and its appliances are the last things to go. With the help of the close-reading questions, students will understand how personification can be used to make abstract ideas seem clear.

Background Have students read the information about Ray Bradbury in the background. Point out that "There Will Come Soft Rains," although set in the future, is deeply rooted in the 1950s, when the world was still reeling from the devastating effects of World War II and the dropping of the atom bomb. It was a time when the war-weary American public rushed to embrace the American Dream and all the technology that went with it, including a wide range of "modern" appliances. Many of Bradbury's stories, including this one, focus on the threat of war and an out-of-control technology.

SETTING A PURPOSE Ask students to pay attention to the way the author uses personification and other figurative language to deliver a strong message about world peace.

Common Core Support

- cite textual evidence
- draw inferences about events based on clues in the text
- analyze how a theme is conveyed through particular details
- determine the meaning of words and phrases, including figurative language

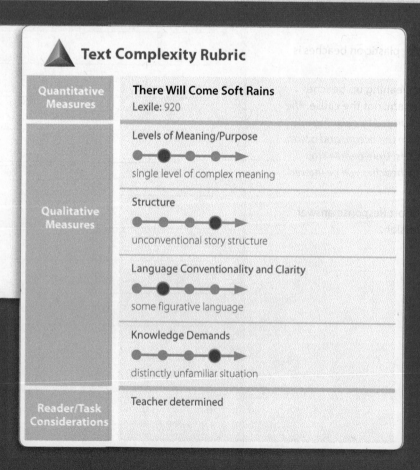

Text Complexity Rubric

There Will Come Soft Rains

Quantitative Measures
Lexile: 920

Qualitative Measures

Levels of Meaning/Purpose
single level of complex meaning

Structure
unconventional story structure

Language Conventionality and Clarity
some figurative language

Knowledge Demands
distinctly unfamiliar situation

Reader/Task Considerations
Teacher determined

Strategies for CLOSE READING

Determine Meanings: Figurative Language

Students should read this story carefully all the way through. Close-reading questions at the bottom of the page will help them understand how the author uses figurative language, including personification, to create meaning. As they read, students should jot down comments or questions about the text in the margins.

WHEN STUDENTS STRUGGLE . . .

To help students understand how personification is used in "There Will Come Soft Rains," have them work in small groups to fill out a chart like the one shown below.

CITE TEXT EVIDENCE For practice in recognizing how the author uses personification, have them find examples in the text and add them to the chart.

Examples of Personification	Effect
". . . the fire in ten billion angry sparks moved with flaming ease from room to room and then up the stairs." (lines 152–153)	The personification of the fire makes it seem cruel and unfeeling; it doesn't care what it destroys.
". . . blind robot faces peered down with faucet mouths gushing green chemical." (lines 166–167)	The robot is dying a slow and painful death; "faucet mouths" allows you to visualize the force of the chemicals it spews.
". . . the stove could be seen making breakfasts at a psychopathic rate . . ." (lines 203–204)	The stove is seen as animate—going crazy as it dies.
"Deep freeze, armchair, film tapes, circuits, beds, and all like skeletons thrown in a cluttered mound deep under . . ." (lines 208–210)	The dying of the house replicates the dying of the people who lived there. The contents of the house are its "bones," which are buried underground.

Background Ray Bradbury *(1920–2012) was born in a small town named Waukegan, Illinois. He was hired to write short stories for a radio show at the age of 14 and joined the Los Angeles Science Fiction Society at the age of 16. In 1953, he published his most famous book,* Fahrenheit 451, *which warned of the dangers of book censorship. In all, Ray Bradbury wrote 27 novels and over 600 short stories.*

There Will Come Soft Rains

Short Story by Ray Bradbury

CLOSE READ
Notes

1. **READ ▷** As you read lines 1–15, begin to collect and cite evidence.

- Underline examples of personification in the text.
- In the margin, define "voice-clock," using clues from the text.
- Circle two phrases that help you infer that no people are in the house.

Ⓐ In the living room the voice-clock sang, *Ticktock, seven o'clock, time to get up, time to get up, seven o'clock!* as if it were afraid that nobody would. The morning house lay empty. The clock ticked on, repeating and repeating its sounds into the emptiness. *Seven-nine, breakfast time, seven-nine!*

In the kitchen the breakfast stove gave a hissing sigh and ejected from its warm interior eight pieces of perfectly browned toast, eight eggs sunny side up, sixteen slices of bacon, and two coffees.

"Today is August 4, 2026," said a second voice from the kitchen
10 ceiling, "in the city of Allendale, California." It repeated the date
Ⓑ three times for memory's sake. "Today is Mr. Featherstone's birthday. Today is the anniversary of Tilita's marriage. Insurance is payable, as are the water, gas, and light bills."

Somewhere in the walls, relays clicked, memory tapes glided under electric eyes.

A voice-clock is a clock that talks.

43

---

1. **READ AND CITE TEXT EVIDENCE**

Ⓐ **ASK STUDENTS** to make an inference about the various types of appliances mentioned. What is their function? *They tell the inhabitants of the house what to do; they give factual information; they keep repeating things over and over.*

CLOSE READ
Notes

Eight-one, tick-tock, eight-one o'clock, off to school, off to work, run, run, eight-one! But no doors slammed, no carpets took the soft tread of rubber heels. It was raining outside. The weather box on the front door sang quietly: "Rain, rain, go away; rubbers, raincoats for today . . ." And the rain tapped on the empty house, echoing.

Outside, the garage chimed and lifted its door to reveal the waiting car. After a long wait the door swung down again.

At eight-thirty the eggs were shriveled and the toast was like stone. An aluminum wedge scraped them into the sink, where hot water whirled them down a metal throat which digested and flushed them away to the distant sea. The dirty dishes were dropped into a hot washer and emerged twinkling dry.

Nine-fifteen, sang the clock, *time to clean.*

Out of **warrens** in the wall, tiny robot mice darted. The rooms were acrawl with the small cleaning animals, all rubber and metal. They thudded against chairs, whirling their moustached runners, kneading the rug nap, sucking gently at hidden dust. Then, like mysterious invaders, they popped into their burrows. Their pink electric eyes faded. The house was clean.

Ten o'clock. The sun came out from behind the rain. The house stood alone in a city of rubble and ashes. This was the one house left standing. At night the ruined city gave off a radioactive glow which could be seen for miles.

The metal throat is a drain in a sink.

warrens:
small, crowded spaces

2. ◀ **REREAD** Reread lines 1–15. What kind of "personality" does the house have? Support your answer with explicit textual evidence.

The house seems like a living thing. It is cheerful and efficient. The clock speaks in rhyme, and the stove cooks a perfect breakfast for four.

3. **READ** ▶ As you read lines 16–38, continue to cite text evidence.

- Underline examples of personification in the text.
- In the margin, explain what the author is referring to when he says "a metal throat."
- Circle what makes the city visible for miles.

44

Ten-fifteen. The garden sprinklers whirled up in golden founts, filling the soft morning air with scatterings of brightness. The water pelted windowpanes, running down the charred west side where the house had been burned evenly free of its white paint. The entire west face of the house was black, save for five places. Here the silhouette in paint of a man mowing a lawn. Here, as in a photograph, a woman bent to pick flowers. Still farther over, their images burned on wood in one titanic instant, a small boy, hands flung into the air; higher up, the image of a thrown ball, and opposite him a girl, hands raised to catch a ball which never came down.

The five spots of paint—the man, the woman, the children, the ball—remained. The rest was a thin charcoaled layer.

The gentle sprinkler rain filled the garden with falling light. Until this day, how well the house had kept its peace. How carefully it had inquired, "Who goes there? What's the password?" and, getting no answer from lonely foxes and whining cats, it had shut up its windows and drawn shades in an old-maidenly preoccupation with self-protection which bordered on a mechanical **paranoia.**

It quivered at each sound, the house did. If a sparrow brushed a window, the shade snapped up. The bird, startled, flew off! No, not even a bird must touch the house!

The boy and the girl were playing catch with a ball.

paranoia:
a psychotic disorder characterized by delusions of persecution

4. ◀ **REREAD** Reread lines 35–38. What conclusion can you draw from the text about what happened to the rest of the houses in the town?

The rest of the houses were probably destroyed by a nuclear weapon—the city "gave off a radioactive glow." The author also refers to the city as "ruined," which would mean something bad had happened.

5. **READ** ▶ As you read lines 39–59, continue to cite text evidence.

- Underline examples of personification in the text.
- In the margin, explain what the boy and girl were doing when the nuclear event occurred.
- Circle the sentence that lets you know something bad is about to happen to the house.

45

---

2. **REREAD AND CITE TEXT EVIDENCE** Have students think about what the house's cheerful, efficient personality suggests about the lives of its inhabitants.

B **ASK STUDENTS** to make an inference about the people from what we know about the house. *The sing-songy repetition of the date (lines 11–12) suggests that the human inhabitants are childlike, and need to be told what to do.*

3. **READ AND CITE TEXT EVIDENCE** The narrator describes breakfast being "whirled down" a metal throat.

C **ASK STUDENTS** why the author used the words *metal throat* to describe a sink drain? What effect does it create? *It makes it seem like the breakfast is being "gobbled up" by the sink.*

Critical Vocabulary: warrens (line 29) Have students explain the meaning of *warrens*. Which word in this paragraph is a synonym of *warrens*? *The word* burrows *(line 33) means the same thing.*

4. **REREAD AND CITE TEXT EVIDENCE** Explain that lines 35–38 tell you that there is only one house left standing, that the rest of the houses have been destroyed.

D **ASK STUDENTS** what they can conclude about the people in the town. *They are all dead.*

5. **READ AND CITE TEXT EVIDENCE** In lines 54–56, the house shuts up its windows and draws its shades in an "old maidenly preoccupation with self-protection."

E **ASK STUDENTS** to explain what the house is reacting to. What causes it to shut down? *There is no response when the house asks for the password, so it shuts down automatically.*

Critical Vocabulary: paranoia (line 56) Have students explain the meaning of *paranoia*. What does this term tell you about the house? *The house is suspicious of everything.*

60   The house was an altar with ten thousand attendants, big, small, servicing, attending, in choirs. But the gods had gone away, and the ritual of the religion continued senselessly, uselessly.

Twelve noon.

A dog whined, shivering, on the front porch.

The front door recognized the dog voice and opened. The dog, once huge and fleshy, but now gone to bone and covered with sores, moved in and through the house, tracking mud. Behind it whirred angry mice, angry at having to pick up mud; angry at inconvenience.

70   For not a leaf fragment blew under the door but what the wall panels flipped open and the copper scrap rats flashed swiftly out. The offending dust, hair, or paper, seized in miniature steel jaws, was raced back to the burrows. There, down tubes which fed into the cellar, it was dropped into the sighing vent of an incinerator which sat like evil Baal[1] in a dark corner.

The dog ran upstairs, hysterically yelping to each door, at last realizing, as the house realized, that only silence was here.

(G)   It sniffed the air and scratched the kitchen door. Behind the door, the stove was making pancakes which filled the house with a rich baked odor and the scent of maple syrup.

80   The dog frothed at the mouth, lying at the door, sniffing, its eyes turned to fire. It ran wildly in circles, biting at its tail, spun in a frenzy, and died. It lay in the parlor for an hour.

Two o'clock, sang a voice.

(H)   Delicately sensing decay at last, the regiments of mice hummed out as softly as blown gray leaves in an electrical wind.

[1] Baal: In the Bible, the god of Canaan, whom the Israelites came to recognize as a false god.

Margin notes (left)

The attendants are the machines in the house; the gods are the people who lived there.

It was looking for its owners, the people who once lived there.

---

6. **◄ REREAD AND DISCUSS** Reread lines 39–50. In a small group, discuss what conclusions you can draw about the nuclear event, based on the silhouettes, or outlines, on the side of the house.

7. **READ ►** As you read lines 60–96, continue to cite text evidence.
   • Underline examples of personification in the text.
   • In the margin, explain who the attendants and gods are.
   • In the margin, explain why the dog yelps at each door.

46

Two-fifteen.

The dog was gone.

In the cellar, the incinerator glowed suddenly and a whirl of sparks leaped up the chimney.

90   *Two thirty-five.*

Bridge[2] tables sprouted from patio walls. Playing cards fluttered onto pads in a shower of pips.[3] Martinis manifested on an oaken bench with egg-salad sandwiches. Music played.

But the tables were silent and the cards untouched.

At four o'clock the tables folded like great butterflies back through the paneled walls.

[2] bridge: a card game.
[3] pips: symbols on the front of a playing card that denote the suit.

---

8. **◄ REREAD** Reread lines 65–89. What inferences can you make about what killed the dog? What happens to the dog's body after it dies? Cite textual evidence to support your inference.

The dog died of radiation poisoning or starvation. It "sniffed the air and scratched the kitchen door" where "the stove was making pancakes which filled the house with a rich baked odor." The dog then "frothed at the mouth" and died. The mice clean up the dog's body, "sensing decay at last," and then they put his body in the incinerator, which "glowed suddenly" while "sparks leaped up the chimney."

47

---

6. **REREAD AND DISCUSS USING TEXT EVIDENCE** Discuss the "five spots of paint" left on the side of the house.

   (F) ASK STUDENTS how these "spots" were created. What details in the text tell you? *The house had been charred on the west side except for places where people had been, where the paint shows through.*

7. **READ AND CITE TEXT EVIDENCE** In this section of text, the dog realizes that there is no one home.

   (G) ASK STUDENTS to make an inference about why the dog thought the people were still at home. What details in the text tell you? *The dog smelled the pancakes that the stove was automatically making* (lines 77–79).

   FOR ELL STUDENTS Some students may be familiar with the adjective *sore*, as in "a sore loser," rather than the noun. Explain that in this context, *sore* means "a painful spot."

8. **REREAD AND CITE TEXT EVIDENCE**

   (H) ASK STUDENTS what they can infer about the way life is valued in this future based on the treatment of the dog. *Students should infer that life is not highly valued. The dog's remains are swept away in a very mechanical fashion and then everyday life proceeds as usual.*

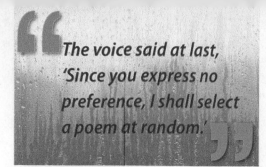

The voice said at last, 'Since you express no preference, I shall select a poem at random.'

Four-thirty.

The nursery walls glowed. Animals took shape: yellow giraffes, blue lions, pink antelopes, lilac panthers cavorting in crystal
100 substance. The walls were glass. They looked out upon color and fantasy. Hidden films clocked through well-oiled sprockets, and the walls lived. The nursery floor was woven to resemble a crisp cereal meadow. Over this ran aluminum roaches and iron crickets, and in the hot, still air butterflies of delicate red tissue wavered among the sharp aromas of animal spoors! There was the sound like a great matted yellow hive of bees within a dark bellows, the lazy bumble of a purring lion. And there was the patter of okapi[4] feet and the murmur of a fresh jungle rain, like other hoofs, falling upon the summer-starched grass. Now the walls dissolved into distances of parched
110 weed, mile on mile, and warm endless sky. The animals drew away into thorn brakes[5] and water holes.

It was the children's hour.

Five o'clock. The bath filled with clear hot water.

Six, seven, eight o'clock. The dinner dishes manipulated like magic tricks, and in the study a *click.* In the metal stand opposite the hearth

---
[4] **okapi:** an animal, similar to a giraffe, with zebra striping.
[5] **thorn brakes:** clumps of thorns; thickets.

---

9. READ ▶ As you read lines 97–140, continue to cite text evidence.

- Underline examples of personification in the text.
- In the margin, explain why "not one will know of the war" (line 132).
- Circle evidence that helps you infer that the animals are not real.

48

---

where a fire now blazed up warmly, a cigar popped out, half an inch of soft gray ash on it, smoking, waiting.

Nine o'clock. The beds warmed their hidden circuits, for nights were cool here.
120 *Nine-five.* A voice spoke from the study ceiling:

"Mrs. McClellan, which poem would you like this evening?"

The house was silent.

The voice said at last, "Since you express no preference, I shall select a poem at random." Quiet music rose to back the voice. "Sara Teasdale. As I recall, your favorite. . . ."

J *There will come soft rains and the smell of the ground,*
And swallows circling with their shimmering sound;

And frogs in the pools singing at night,
And wild plum trees in **tremulous** *white;*

130 *Robins will wear their feathery fire,*
Whistling their whims on a low fence-wire;

I *And not one will know of the war, not one*
Will care at last when it is done.

Not one would mind, neither bird nor tree,
If mankind perished utterly;

And Spring herself, when she woke at dawn
Would scarcely know that we were gone."

The fire burned on the stone hearth, and the cigar fell away into a mound of quiet ash on its tray. The empty chairs faced each other
140 between the silent walls, and the music played.

K At ten o'clock the house began to die.

The wind blew. A falling tree bough crashed through the kitchen window. Cleaning solvent, bottled, shattered over the stove. The room was ablaze in an instant!

tremulous:
quivering; shaking

The animals and plants will not realize that there were once people, before a war.

---

10. ◀ REREAD AND DISCUSS Reread lines 126–137. The title of this poem is "There Will Come Soft Rains." In a small group, discuss why Bradbury might have borrowed this title for his story.

11. READ ▶ As you read lines 141–189, continue to cite evidence.

- Underline examples of personification in the text.
- In the margin, explain what the "twenty snakes" are.
- Circle the names of parts of the body.

49

---

9. READ AND CITE TEXT EVIDENCE Have students revisit lines 132–137 from Teasdale's poem.

I **ASK STUDENTS** to explain what these lines of poetry have to do with the rest of the story. Why does the author include them here? *They address the present situation. The author is saying that no one will remember our world or care that it is gone.*

FOR ELL STUDENTS Explain that a sprocket is a toothed wheel that helps a mechanism or another wheel move. Ask for a volunteer to give you examples of machines that may have this kind of wheel.

10. REREAD AND DISCUSS USING TEXT EVIDENCE

J **ASK STUDENTS** to reread lines 126–129 to hear the words "There will come soft rains" in context. Have them discuss what the title says about Bradbury's vision of the world after it destroys itself. What will it look like? *Bradbury sees it as a paradise with no memory of anything having existed before.*

11. READ AND CITE TEXT EVIDENCE Have students note that *personification* in this section refers to death and dying.

K **ASK STUDENTS** how the author uses personification to make the death of the house more vivid. *He "humanizes" it by using words that refer to parts of the body.*

Critical Vocabulary: tremulous (line 129) Have students explain the meaning of *tremulous.* How does this word help you visualize the plum trees? *The trees are hopeful as new brides.*

"Fire!" screamed a voice. The house lights flashed, water pumps shot water from the ceilings. But the solvent spread on the linoleum, licking, eating, under the kitchen door, while the voices took it up in chorus: "Fire, fire, fire!"

The house tried to save itself. Doors sprang tightly shut, but the windows were broken by the heat and the wind blew and sucked upon the fire.

The house gave ground as the fire in ten billion angry sparks moved with flaming ease from room to room and then up the stairs. While scurrying water rats squeaked from the walls, pistoled their water, and ran for more. And the wall sprays let down showers of mechanical rain.

But too late. Somewhere, sighing, a pump shrugged to a stop. The quenching rain ceased. The reserve water supply which had filled baths and washed dishes for many quiet days was gone.

The fire crackled up the stairs. It fed upon Picassos and Matisses in the upper halls, like delicacies, baking off the oily flesh, tenderly crisping the canvases into black shavings.

Now the fire lay in beds, stood in windows, changed the colors of drapes!

And then, reinforcements.

From attic trapdoors, blind robot faces peered down with faucet mouths gushing green chemical.

The fire backed off, as even an elephant must at the sight of a dead snake. Now there were twenty snakes whipping over the floor, killing the fire with a clear cold venom of green froth.

But the fire was clever. It had sent flame outside the house, up through the attic to the pumps there. An explosion! The attic brain which directed the pumps was shattered into bronze shrapnel on the beams.

The fire rushed back into every closet and felt of the clothes hung there.

The house shuddered, oak bone on bone, its bared skeleton cringing from the heat, its wire, its nerves revealed as if a surgeon had

The twenty snakes are a green chemical meant to put out the fire.

torn the skin off to let the red veins and capillaries quiver in the scalded air. Help, help! Fire! Run, run! Heat snapped mirrors like the first brittle winter ice. And the voices wailed, Fire, fire, run, run, like a tragic nursery rhyme, a dozen voices, high, low, like children dying in a forest, alone, alone. And the voices fading as the wires popped their sheathings like hot chestnuts. One, two, three, four, five voices died.

In the nursery the jungle burned. Blue lions roared, purple giraffes bounded off. The panthers ran in circles, changing color, and ten million animals, running before the fire, vanished off toward a distant steaming river. . . .

Ten more voices died. In the last instant under the fire avalanche, other choruses, **oblivious**, could be heard announcing the time, playing music, cutting the lawn by remote-control mower, or setting an umbrella frantically out and in, the slamming and opening front door, a thousand things happening, like a clock shop when each clock strikes the hour insanely before or after the other, a scene of maniac confusion, yet unity; singing, screaming, a few last cleaning mice darting bravely out to carry the horrid ashes away! And one voice, with **sublime** disregard for the situation, read poetry aloud in the fiery study, until all the film spools burned, until all the wires withered and the circuits cracked.

The fire burst the house and let it slam flat down, puffing out skirts of spark and smoke.

In the kitchen, an instant before the rain of fire and timber, the stove could be seen making breakfasts at a psychopathic rate, ten dozen eggs, six loaves of toast, twenty dozen bacon strips, which, eaten by fire, started the stove working again, hysterically hissing!

oblivious:
unknowing

sublime:
excellent

The stove makes breakfast.

12. ◀ **REREAD AND DISCUSS** Reread lines 149–185. In a small group, discuss the ways in which the "personalities" of the fire and the house create an impression of war.

13. **READ** ▶ As you read lines 190–216, continue to cite text evidence.

- Underline examples of personification.
- In the margin, describe two actions that happen at both the beginning and the end of the story.

12. REREAD AND DISCUSS USING TEXT EVIDENCE

L **ASK STUDENTS** to cite examples of personification used to describe the cruelty of the fire. *Students may cite "angry sparks"; "crackled up the stairs"; "fed upon" paintings like they were "delicacies . . . tenderly crisping the canvases into black shavings."*

13. READ AND CITE TEXT EVIDENCE

M **ASK STUDENTS** to discuss the behavior of the mechanical appliances. What does it say about machines? *They are unthinking and unfeeling; they do what they're programmed to do.*

Critical Vocabulary: oblivious (line 191) Why does the author describe the machines as oblivious? *The machines don't care about anything.*

Critical Vocabulary: sublime (line 198) What does "sublime disregard" say about the voice of the poetry reader? *It is too "refined" to notice that everything around it is on fire.*

CLOSE READ
Notes

The crash. The attic smashing into kitchen and parlor. The parlor into cellar, cellar into subcellar. Deep freeze, armchair, film tapes, circuits, beds, and all like skeletons thrown in a cluttered mound deep
210 under.

Smoke and silence. A great quantity of smoke.

Dawn showed faintly in the east. Among the ruins, one wall stood alone. Within the wall, a last voice said, over and over again and again, even as the sun rose to shine upon the heaped rubble and steam:

"Today is August 5, 2026, today is August 5, 2026, today is . . ."

The voice-clock announces the date.

14. **◄ REREAD AND DISCUSS** Reread lines 212–216. In a small group, discuss your responses to the ending. What is ironic, or unexpected, about the way the story ends?

SHORT RESPONSE

Cite Text Evidence What overall effect does the author's personification of the house have on the reader as the house burns down? **Cite text evidence** to support your ideas.

When the writer says "The house tried to save itself," it almost feels like the house literally made the choice to defend itself. The house falling apart makes the reader empathize—it's like a person is dying. The author compares parts of the house to a human body, as when he refers to the "attic brain" being "shattered" or when he says "its nerves revealed as if a surgeon had torn the skin off" when referring to the wiring.

52

---

14. **REREAD AND DISCUSS USING TEXT EVIDENCE** Have students discuss the end of the world as depicted in lines 207–215.

 ASK STUDENTS to cite evidence showing that technology outlives humans. *They may note that the date has moved ahead another day (it is now August 5), but the people have not.*

SHORT RESPONSE

Cite Text Evidence Students' responses should include text evidence that supports their positions. They should:

- cite examples of personification and other figures of speech.
- draw conclusions about the story's theme.
- examine the effect of word choice on meaning.
- make inferences about events and characters.

TO CHALLENGE STUDENTS . . .

To help students deepen their understanding of Bradbury's writing, tell them that he has often speculated in writing on the impact of future technology on the world.

ASK STUDENTS to find out more about Bradbury's views of technology. Have them research the following questions:

- What does Bradbury think of the Internet, the automobile, virtual reality, and other inventions?
- Which elements of some of his stories and other writings actually predicted some aspect of the future?
- Which elements were way off the mark?

After students have completed their research, have them present their findings about Bradbury's views and writings to the class.

DIG DEEPER

1. With the class, return to Question 3, Read. Have students share their responses.

   ASK STUDENTS to think about the role of the machines in the story.

   - Students can make inferences about how this technology would affect people's daily lives. What does it say about the importance of the individual in this society? What does it say about free will?

   - Students can list the machines' directives and messages and write a description of each. What does this suggest about who's in charge? Why might they want people to listen to these messages all day long?

   - Have students consider a society completely run by machines. Is that in our future? What can we do to prevent Bradbury's dark vision from becoming a reality? Is there a connection between war and the use of technology?

2. With the class, return to Question 5, Read. Have students share their responses.

   - Have students make inferences how people's lives were affected by the war. What does the house's "preoccupation with self-protection" suggest about people's state of mind? Why was it so important to be barricaded from the outside world? What inferences can they make from the necessity of a password?

   - Have students think about how the climate of paranoia affected people's relationships with each other.

3. With the class, return to Question 9, Read. Have students share their responses.

   - Have students analyze Teasdale's poem. What common threads can they find?

   - Have students find similarities between the poem and the story. Have them analyze their common threads. How do the authors attempt to convey their messages?

   ASK STUDENTS to return to their Short Response answer and revise it based on the class discussion.

CLOSE READING NOTES

On the Titanic, Defined by What They Wore

Newspaper Article by Guy Trebay

Why This Text

Students do not always take the time to analyze the meanings of words and phrases as they are used in a text. Newspaper articles like this one by Guy Trebay include key ideas and word choices that must be analyzed to be understood. With the help of the close-reading questions, students will analyze Trebay's key ideas and word choices. This close reading will help students understand the content of the article.

Background Have students read the background information. Introduce the selection by telling students that the *Titanic* was a brand new ship that was built with new technology, such as electric watertight doors. Many people believed the ship could not sink. Maybe that explains why there were not enough lifeboats on board and so many people died. Tell students that Guy Trebay is an award-winning style writer for the *New York Times*.

SETTING A PURPOSE Ask students to look up words they do not know. Does analyzing the meanings of words and phrases help them understand what they are reading?

 Common Core Support

- cite textual evidence
- analyze how a key idea is introduced
- determine the meaning of words and phrases as they are used in a text
- integrate information presented in different formats

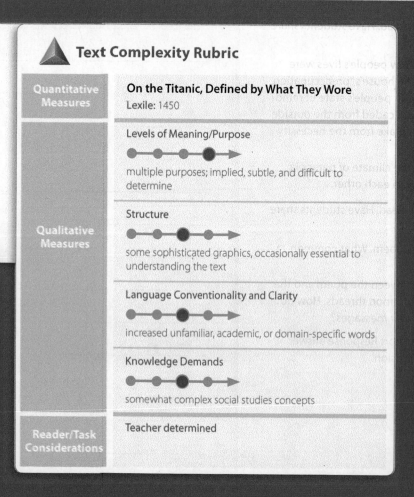

Text Complexity Rubric

Quantitative Measures

On the Titanic, Defined by What They Wore
Lexile: 1450

Qualitative Measures

Levels of Meaning/Purpose

multiple purposes; implied, subtle, and difficult to determine

Structure

some sophisticated graphics, occasionally essential to understanding the text

Language Conventionality and Clarity

increased unfamiliar, academic, or domain-specific words

Knowledge Demands

somewhat complex social studies concepts

Reader/Task Considerations

Teacher determined

Strategies for CLOSE READING

Analyze Meanings of Words and Phrases

Students should read this newspaper article carefully all the way through. Close-reading questions at the bottom of the page will help them focus on a thorough analysis of the text. As they read, students should jot down comments or questions about the article in the side margins.

WHEN STUDENTS STRUGGLE . . .

To help students analyze the meanings of words and phrases, have them work in a small group to fill out a chart, such as the one shown below, as they analyze the text.

CITE TEXT EVIDENCE For practice in analyzing words and phrases as they are used in a text, ask students to cite sentences that contain powerful verbs, vivid adjectives, or precise nouns; define the specific word; and explain Trebay's use of the word in the text.

| sentence with specific word: "Tatters and scraps, they emerged from the deep coated with mire and miraculously although tenuously intact." (lines 1–2) | ▶ | definition: tenuously, adverb: without much substance or strength | ▶ | Trebay's use of the word: Trebay lets readers know that the clothes that were recovered from the Titanic were barely intact and could easily fall apart or be destroyed. |
| sentence with specific word: | ▶ | definition: | ▶ | Trebay's use of the word: |

Background *On April 10th, 1912, the RMS Titanic left Southampton, England, for New York City on its first and only voyage. The Titanic had been called "unsinkable" and was the most luxurious passenger liner of its day. On April 15th, the ship collided with an iceberg and sank. Over 1,500 people died in the freezing waters. The wreckage was discovered in 1985, but the ship remains on the ocean floor to this day. The Titanic has been immortalized through film, books, television series, songs, exhibits—and in this recent newspaper article.*

On the Titanic, Defined by What They Wore

Newspaper Article by Guy Trebay

CLOSE READ
Notes

1. **READ ▶** As you read lines 1–34, begin to cite text evidence.
   - In the margin, explain what you think the article's title means.
   - In the margin, paraphrase what the second sentence says.
   - Underline items recovered from the *Titanic*.

Tatters and scraps, they emerged from the deep coated with mire and miraculously although tenuously intact. Treated with the reverence due relics of perhaps the greatest maritime tragedy and with all the care modern conservation science could summon, they were restored, put on display and then offered this week in an exceptional single-lot auction of the more than 5,000 objects (with a current estimated worth of $190 million) that salvagers of the Titanic found scattered across the North Atlantic seabed.

10 A surprising amount of ephemera[1] defied logic to survive the sinking of the unsinkable ocean liner that went to the bottom 100 years ago on April 15.

Most astonishing of all the recovered items, it would seem, were the articles of clothing either carried or worn by passengers before the 882-foot-long liner sank in icy water. The ship broke apart and shot to

---
[1] **ephemera:** things that are useful for only a short time.

Passengers on the Titanic wore distinctive clothing.

More than 5,000 restored objects salvaged from the Titanic, valued at $190 million, were put up for auction.

53

---

1. **READ AND CITE TEXT EVIDENCE** Discuss the meaning of the word *salvagers* (line 7).

A **ASK STUDENTS** to read aloud their paraphrase of the second sentence to a partner. Have them work with their partner to improve their paraphrase and include text evidence. *Students should cite evidence of the auction (line 6) and should cite the "5,000 objects . . . that salvagers of the Titanic found . . .," (lines 6–7).* Have them underline examples of some of the 5,000 objects up for auction.

the bottom; its contents fell more slowly, fluttering to the depths like grim leaf fall.

And there, in the lightless saline netherworld, a vest, a trilby hat, a pair of laced boots, a belted valise and an alligator bag (along with a huge range of artifacts) lay scattered across a broad apron of
20 remnants.

The wreck was discovered in 1985 and the objects were brought to the surface over the course of seven **expeditions.** Perhaps more than the teacups or perfume flacons, the garments eerily conjure lives lost

B that clear April night, so much so that when the Academy Award-winning designer Deborah L. Scott prepared to create costumes for James Cameron's blockbuster 1997 film "Titanic," she covered her office walls with photographs of the Titanic's passengers to absorb the sartorial[2] elements that enliven character.

The removable celluloid collars with laundry marks inside, the
30 man's vest with a single vertical buttonhole for a watch chain and fob, the homespun finery packed away by village girls as a trousseau[3] for an imaginary future: these sorts of detail were employed by Ms. Scott to summon the beings who once inhabited garments that in some cases, though it is hard to imagine, survived their owners.

Consider, for instance, Marion Meanwell's handbag.

Using public records, newspaper accounts at the time and the recollections of survivors, historians like Richard Davenport-Hines, author of "Voyagers of the Titanic: Passengers, Sailors, Shipbuilders,

---
[2] sartorial: related to clothing.
[3] trousseau: a bride's personal possessions.

---

2. ◀ REREAD Reread lines 21–34. Where did Deborah L. Scott find inspiration for her costume designs for the 1997 movie?

She used pictures of Titanic passengers to get the feeling of the kinds of clothing they typically wore.

3. READ ▶ As you read lines 35–80, continue to cite text evidence.
• In the margin, paraphrase the quote at the top of the next page.
• Underline information that helps you understand Mrs. Meanwell's story.
• In the margin, explain why it was so important to have credentials.

54

> **As was true of many ocean voyagers of the time, Mrs. Meanwell was on a passage intended to be a momentous alteration of a settled life.**

Aristocrats, and the Worlds They Came From," have pieced together
40 fragmentary biographies of victims like Mrs. Meanwell (nee Ogden), a
C British milliner[4] traveling aboard the Titanic on a third-class ticket.

As was true of many ocean voyagers of the time, Mrs. Meanwell was on a passage intended to be a momentous alteration of a settled life. First chartered to sail on the liner Majestic, Mrs. Meanwell
D rebooked on the Titanic after that vessel was removed from regular service. Tucked into her handbag were a number of documents, among them a letter from the London landlords Wheeler Sons & Co.

This **innocuous** note, stating blandly that "we have always found Meanwell a good tenant and prompt in payment of her rent," carried
50 an extra freight of meaning for an immigrant hoping to build a new life.

"If you were coming over without **credentials** or with no prospect of work," Mr. Davenport-Hines said, it was not uncommon for examiners at Ellis Island to refuse entry to new arrivals and to send them home as "vagrants or tramps."

Then as now, an alligator bag was a luxury item, a satchel of substance carried by a woman whose own social authority it advertised. Mrs. Meanwell was parted from her alligator bag on the night the Titanic sank and, while she perished, her purse did not.

---
[4] milliner: hatmaker.

55

---

2. REREAD AND CITE TEXT EVIDENCE

B ASK STUDENTS to cite text evidence to support their answer. *Students should cite text from lines 24–27, "when . . . Scott prepared to create costumes for . . . 'Titanic' she covered her office walls with photographs of the Titanic's passengers . . ."*

3. READ AND CITE TEXT EVIDENCE

C ASK STUDENTS to cite textual evidence that helps them understand Marion Meanwell's story. *Students should underline evidence about Meanwell's background, (lines 41 and 65), her plans (lines 42–44 and 65–67), and evidence of the credentials she carried in her handbag (lines 48–49).*

Critical Vocabulary: expedition (line 22) Have students define *expedition* as Trebay uses it here. *Students should explain that these expeditions are journeys to the sunken Titanic.*

Critical Vocabulary: innocuous (line 48) Ask students to compare their definitions. Why does Trebay describe the note as innocuous? *Students should recognize that Trebay is drawing attention to the contrast between how plain the note might seem to us today and how important it was to Meanwell, as well as what a meaningful clue it was to Meanwell's story.*

Critical Vocabulary: credentials (line 52) Have students share their definitions. Did Mrs. Meanwell have credentials? What did she have? *She had a letter from her landlord, her marriage license, and her parents' wedding license.*

60 "Inside it was her marriage license, as well as her parents' wedding license," said David Galusha, a conservator for Premier Exhibition, the Atlanta-based company that sold the Titanic relics, along with the video archives of its salvage expeditions and the intellectual rights to create objects using the R.M.S. Titanic "brand."

"She had sold everything, was a widow and was moving to the United States to be with her daughter, who had two children, to assist with them," Mr. Galusha said of Mrs. Meanwell.

That the bag survived was owed in part to the fact that the objects scattered from the wreck spent the last century, "two-miles down, in
70 an environment with no light, and hardly any oxygen," the conservator said. There was something else. "The thickness of the alligator skin, the quality, is no comparison to what you would find today," Mr. Galusha said. "There was a general attitude at the time of making things durable, things that would stand the test of time."

That they did so is an unexpectedly moving aspect of a tale so often rehearsed that its human dimensions are sometimes overlooked. "Titanic" may be, as some claim, one of the most universally recognized names in the English language. Yet the lives at the heart of the story are easily forgotten, transformed into facile metaphors and
80 symbols of gender and class.

4. **◀ REREAD** Reread lines 42–80. Why does the author include the narrative history about Mrs. Meanwell? Cite text evidence in your response.

The story of Mrs. Meanwell represents one of the "lives at the heart" of the history of the Titanic. The details of her life are remembered thanks to the study of "a number of documents" recovered from her alligator handbag.

5. **READ ▶** As you read lines 81–114, continue to cite text evidence.
- Underline the role that clothing played after the *Titanic* sank.
- In the margin, explain what the names of first-class passengers reveal about the gap between social classes.
- In the margin, paraphrase what Cohen says about the *Titanic* as a stage.

56

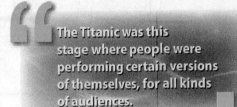

The Titanic was this stage where people were performing certain versions of themselves, for all kinds of audiences.

E There is the tragic noblesse of the first-class passengers, people named Straus and Widener and Guggenheim; the hopeless scrabbling of the businessmen and boys traveling in second class, some kept at gunpoint from entering lifeboats that went off half-filled; and the wretched doom of those nameless victims at the bottom of the social scale.

"They were all judged finally on their clothes and the quality of their clothes," Mr. Davenport-Hines said, adding that among the aspects of the story most laden with pathos is the contemporary
90 depiction of bodies frozen into life jackets and hauled from the North Atlantic and sorted by class, largely according to what else they had on.

Clothes, said Lisa Cohen, a biographer whose book "All We Know" delineates the lives of three early modernist women—Mercedes de Acosta, Madge Garland, Esther Murphy—in part by using the "soft history" of fashion to demonstrate that our surfaces **elucidate** "our depths," as the author said.

The identity masquerade that artists like Cindy Sherman explore to theatrical effect was on prominent view aboard the floating theater
100 of an ocean passage, Ms. Cohen said. The Titanic was in that sense a stage prop moving across what was by all accounts a flat and unthreatening ocean and also across the proscenium[5] of a new century.

F "The Titanic was this stage where people were performing certain versions of themselves, for all kinds of audiences," Ms. Cohen said. "It was a transitional space in a transitional period, a time of self-invention right before the war."

[5] **proscenium:** the part of the stage in front of the curtain.

First-class passengers are remembered by name, as individuals, but the lower classes are nameless.

elucidate: explain

The Titanic was the stage, and the passengers were performers.

57

---

4. **REREAD AND CITE TEXT EVIDENCE**

D ASK STUDENTS to cite text evidence to support their explanation of why the author chose to include the narrative history about Mrs. Meanwell. *Answers will vary. Students may cite that her story represents one of the "lives at the heart" of the history of the Titanic (line 78), or that "a number of documents" in her handbag revealed details of her life (line 46).*

5. **READ AND CITE TEXT EVIDENCE**

E ASK STUDENTS to cite text evidence to support their explanation of what the names of first-class passengers reveal about the gap between social classes. *Students should cite evidence from lines 81–86.*

FOR ELL STUDENTS Don't let students confuse *conservator* and *conservative*. Explain that a conservator is a person responsible for items in an exhibit or museum, while *conservative* usually describes traditional views, and the opposition to severe change.

Critical Vocabulary: elucidate (line 97) Ask students to compare their definitions of *elucidate*. Then have them define the related word *lucid*. Discuss connotations of the word *elucidate* and why Trebay chose this word.

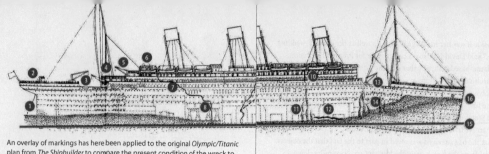

An overlay of markings has here been applied to the original *Olympic/Titanic* plan from *The Shipbuilder* to compare the present condition of the wreck to the ship as her builders conceived her.

1 Rudder buried 45 feet.   **2** Poop Deck peeled back over stern.
3 After Well Deck torn away.   **4** Decks collapsed and compressed.
5 Starboard A-Deck cargo crane wrenched but still fitted.   **6** Second-class entrance and elevator housing remain.
7 Decks collapsed down.   **8** Deck rests on cylinder heads of reciprocating engines.

9 Shell plating remains partially upright although Boat Deck is angled down in center.   **10** One-foot gap in expansion joint.
11 Hull buckled below expansion joint.   **12** Possible iceberg damage here.
13 Bow angled downward.   **14** Buckling caused by angle of bow.
15 Level of original keel.   **16** Bow plowed in over 60 feet.

nuanced:
subtle,
detailed

Fixed and flattened in memory by the shock of disaster, the realities of the Titanic become available to **nuanced** interpretation
110 only now, a century later, just as with the sale this week of the hats and vests and shoes and watches saved from the ocean, come into wider view.

"It's the power of the surface that's so beautiful here," Ms. Cohen said. "The smallest detail reveals so much."

At a minimum, the sartorial details convey some overlooked information: people were generally smaller in 1912, had tidier heads, more-compact torsos, less-capacious lungs.

6. ◀ **REREAD AND DISCUSS** Reread lines 98–114. With a small group, discuss the many ways in which the *Titanic* was a "stage." In what ways were the passengers' clothing like costumes?

7. **READ** ▶ As you read lines 115–148, continue to cite text evidence.

• Circle two examples of recovered clothing.
• In the margin, explain what the recovered clothing teaches about people of the past.
• Underline text that shows how people—on screen and in real life—make a statement with clothing.

58

"Take (the trilby,) Mr. Galusha, the conservator, said, referring to a felt hat that emerged from conservation in such pristine condition
120 that "it could literally be worn right now," although only by a woman with a small head.

"There's a C.S.I.[6] side of this story," he said. The size of the hat tacitly points to shifts in diet over the last century, to the introduction of antibiotics and vitamins. "On average, the size of our rib cages increases 4 percent per generation," Mr. Galusha said, a claim that would go a long way toward explaining why the contemporary bride can't fit into her grandmother's wedding gown.

People were frugal in 1912, or anyway less accustomed to the ease of disposable fashion. A patch of "invisible" weaving can still be
130 detected in a custom-made (gentleman's suit) recovered from the Titanic wreckage. "It was a good suit, and instead of discarding the trousers, the owner had the hole repaired," Mr. Galusha said.

_____
[6] C.S.I.: Crime Scene Investigation.

The clothing shows how people's bodies have changed over time, becoming larger.

8. ◀ **REREAD AND DISCUSS** Review the diagram of the *Titanic*. With a small group, discuss what the diagram shows.

59

6. **REREAD AND DISCUSS USING TEXT EVIDENCE**

F **ASK STUDENTS** to cite specific text evidence in their discussion, with line numbers and references to support their conclusions. *Students should cite line 104 and note that clothes were part of people's attempts at "performing certain versions of themselves…"*

7. **READ AND CITE TEXT EVIDENCE**

G **ASK STUDENTS** to cite text evidence to support their explanation of what the recovered clothing teaches about people of the past. *Students should cite lines 122–127 as evidence that people's bodies have changed over time, becoming larger.*

Critical Vocabulary: nuanced (line 109) Ask volunteers to read their definitions of *nuanced*. Ask students to explain the meaning of *nuanced* as it is used here.

8. **REREAD AND DISCUSS USING TEXT EVIDENCE**

H **ASK STUDENTS** to appoint a reporter for each group to explain what happened to the ship at the numbered locations on the diagram. Students should describe the damage to such parts of the ship as the various decks, the hull, the rudder, and the bow.

FOR ELL STUDENTS Explain the word *frugal*. Tell students that frugal people are careful about spending money on things they don't really need. Encourage students to give you an example of what a frugal person might do.

Critical Vocabulary: amalgam (line 145) Ask students to explain the meaning of *amalgam* as it is used here. In what way are clothes an amalgam? *They are a mixture of various fabrics, colors, and styles.*

54

CLOSE READ
Notes

Though they largely passed into legend, those who lost their lives in the epoch-making shipwreck were never "characters," said Deborah Nadoolman Landis, the curator of "Hollywood Costume," an exhibition exploring the role costume design plays in cinema history that will open in October at the Victoria and Albert Museum in London. "A character is a pretend person, and real people lost their lives," in the wreck of the Titanic, said Ms. Landis, an Academy
140 Award-nominated designer. <u>On-screen, their clothes served a crucial function, as flashcard symbols of social identity.</u> "One of the ways you make people real in movies is through clothes."

People are to a surprising extent what they imagine themselves to be every time they get dressed, Ms. Landis said. "<u>Our clothing is an **amalgam** of what we are: the shoes, the vest, the trousers, the suit jacket purchased at different times</u>," she said. "<u>Clothes hold us together in so many ways.</u> They're the closest thing to our bodies, our pulse."

amalgam:
mixture

SHORT RESPONSE

Cite Text Evidence What information in the article and the diagram helps you understand how the trip was different for first-class passengers and steerage passengers of the *Titanic*? Be sure to **cite text evidence** from the diagram in your response.

The diagram shows that there were separate entrances for the different classes (for example, the second-class entrance is shown in the diagram). These entrances went to different deck levels, which were separate for the different classes. People were identified by the clothing they wore or the items they brought with them, but they were also identified by where they were situated on the ship. They were not only separated by the quality of the clothes they wore— they were physically separated from one another by location.

60

TO CHALLENGE STUDENTS . . .

For more context and historical background, students can view the video "Titanic at 100: Mystery Solved" in their eBooks.

ASK STUDENTS to use the newspaper article by Trebay as well as the audio and video evidence to write a paragraph describing the sinking of the *Titanic*. *Students should write paragraphs that include descriptive details of the events as they are described in the article and the video.*

DIG DEEPER

With the class, return to Question 8, Reread and Discuss. Have students share the results of their discussion.

ASK STUDENTS whether they were satisfied with the outcome of their small-group discussions. Have each group share their review of the diagram. What text evidence can they identify that supports their review?

- Encourage students to tell whether there was any disagreement about what the diagram shows. Did examining the diagram closely and discussing evidence help to resolve the disagreement?

- Have groups explore the text for further evidence that supports what they found in the diagram.

- After students have shared the results of their group's discussion, ask whether another group found evidence they would like to include in their findings.

ASK STUDENTS to return to their Short Response answer and revise it based on the class discussion.

SHORT RESPONSE

Cite Text Evidence Student responses will vary, but they should cite evidence from the article to support their comparison. Students should:

- compare the experience of first-class and steerage passengers on the *Titanic*.

- cite evidence from the text.

- cite evidence from the diagram.

Making Your Voice Heard

Making Your Voice Heard

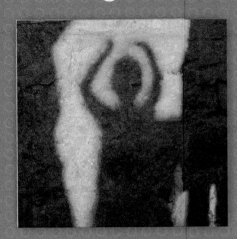

"When people don't express themselves,
they die one piece at a time."

—Laurie Halse Anderson

INFORMATIONAL TEXTS

Views on Zoos

SHORT STORY

What Do Fish Have to Do with Anything?   Avi

Views on Zoos

Why This Text

It might be difficult for students to evaluate arguments with different points of view, or to identify the reasons and evidence a writer uses to support a case. In "Views on Zoos," students will compare and contrast different viewpoints on the same subject, taking into account supporting evidence and the writer's use of persuasive techniques. With the help of the close-reading questions, students will determine the validity of each writer's claim based on a set of objective criteria.

Background Have students read the background information about zoos. Point out that in "Views on Zoos," they will read various arguments for and against zoos. Point out, however, that there are many kinds of zoos, and not all of them are featured in the article. There are urban and suburban zoos, sprawling open-air zoos, safari parks, game reserves, and petting zoos. There are even zoos dedicated to exhibiting one animal species alone. At the Jurong Bird Park in Singapore, there are more than 1,000 flamingoes living in a sprawling African-wetlands habitat, where they are treated to a daily simulated thunderstorm!

SETTING A PURPOSE Ask students to pay attention to the way the writers use loaded language and other persuasive techniques to strengthen their arguments.

Common Core Support

- cite textual evidence
- determine an author's point of view in a text
- trace and evaluate the argument and specific claims in a text
- compare and contrast

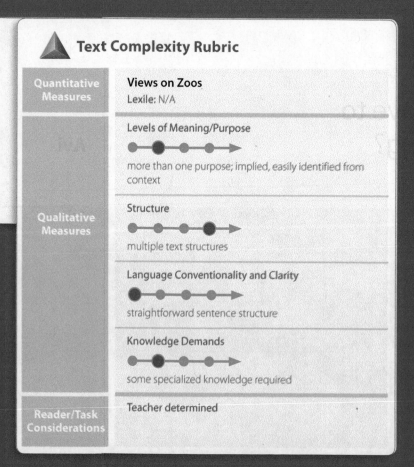

Text Complexity Rubric

Quantitative Measures	**Views on Zoos** Lexile: N/A
Qualitative Measures	**Levels of Meaning/Purpose** more than one purpose; implied, easily identified from context
	Structure multiple text structures
	Language Conventionality and Clarity straightforward sentence structure
	Knowledge Demands some specialized knowledge required
Reader/Task Considerations	Teacher determined

Strategies for CLOSE READING

Compare and Contrast: Arguments

Students should read the texts carefully all the way through. Close-reading questions at the bottom of the page will help them understand how a writer uses persuasive techniques to make an argument. As they read, students should jot down comments or questions about the text in the margins.

WHEN STUDENTS STRUGGLE . . .

To help students analyze and compare arguments, have them work in small groups to fill out a chart like the one shown below.

CITE TEXT EVIDENCE For practice in identifying evidence supporting an argument, have students cite evidence from the texts for and against the existence of zoos.

Evidence for Zoos	Evidence Against Zoos
"Animals that are constantly . . . life on this planet." (Functions of a Zoo, lines 3–14)	"I couldn't help noticing . . . they seemed defeated." (Sonia's Blog, lines 21–23)
"I loved seeing the animals." (Sonia's Blog, line 32)	"I felt bad . . . they couldn't be themselves." (Sonia's Blog, lines 33–34)
"Zoo conditions for animals have improved vastly." (Innocent and Imprisoned, line 8)	"The zoo inmates are all innocent." (Innocent and Imprisoned, line 7)
"Zoos also provide their customers an education." (Innocent and Imprisoned, line 29)	"Information gained from . . . in unnatural situations." (Innocent and Imprisoned, lines 27–28)

Background *The oldest known zoo existed in Hierakonpolis, Egypt, more than 5,500 years ago. It had hippos, elephants, baboons, and wildcats. In ancient times, a zoo was meant to display a leader's power and wealth. The purpose of today's zoos is different. For example, when the popular and vast Bronx Zoo opened in 1899, its purpose was to preserve native animals and promote zoology. Today, some people question whether zoos should exist at all.*

Views on Zoos

CLOSE READ Notes

1. **READ ▷** As you read lines 1–14, begin to collect and cite evidence.
- Circle the main functions of a zoo.
- Underline an example of each function (lines 3–14).
- In the margin, summarize the functions of a zoo.

Functions of a Zoo

A Zoo **advocates** call attention to the main functions of a zoo: conservation, education and research, and recreation.

- Animals that are constantly threatened in the wild are safe in a zoo, and they are well-fed and have medical care. Animals that are endangered can be bred in captivity, ensuring that their species do not die out.

B • It is difficult to study animals in the wild; they are generally shy of humans and will avoid all contact. In the confines of a zoo enclosure, animal behavior can be studied. Animal responses to various conditions can be analyzed.

10

- Human beings have a natural curiosity about animals. Millions of people who otherwise could observe only a few animals in their lives can visit a zoo and marvel at the diversity of life on this planet.

advocates:
supporters

Zoos protect animals, let us learn about them, and provide a place to have fun.

63

1. **READ AND CITE TEXT EVIDENCE** Have students think about the three main functions of a zoo.

A **ASK STUDENTS** to tell which function is primarily devoted to helping animals. *Students should cite protection of animals.* Which is primarily devoted to helping humans? *Students should cite providing a place to have fun.*

Critical Vocabulary: advocates (line 1) Have students share their definitions. What does a human rights advocate do? *A human rights advocate works to support human rights.*

Sonia's Blog

Who I Am, What I Do—Every Day

Saturday, June 18

The zoo! I visited the zoo with mom today. It's the same zoo she visited with her Mom. Mom said she remembers that the first thing you would see was a cage with two Siberian[1] tigers in it. But now the tigers have a new home, a huge area about the size of three football fields. They need it—they are huge themselves. One of the tigers weighs more than 600 pounds! They are my absolute favorite animals there. Go on the web and find some images of them, you'll understand.

We couldn't see everything in just one day, and luckily Mom and I both like the same animals. That means no snakes or insects! I always say I like all animals, so I'm a bit embarrassed to admit that I prefer the furry, cuddly ones (but when a tiger looks you in the eye, you know it isn't very cuddly).

There were elephants (cuddly?) and giraffes! Hippos! Monkeys of all kinds! I started wondering where they all came

---
[1] **Siberian:** from a region in northern Russia.

The entry is about going to the zoo.

D

10

---

from, and how they liked it here. I talked to some zookeepers. I guess it's obvious, but they all love animals, too. They take good care of them, and know each one's personality. But I couldn't help noticing a sad look in some of the animals' eyes. And they seemed defeated.

I can go jogging all around the pond and across the park, and then go with Mom to our friends way across town just to visit, that's what I can do. And then come home, and go to school the next day. Some of the animals had a faraway look that seemed to say how far they wanted to go, too. One of the keepers told me that a Siberian tiger (I know, I can't stop talking about those giant cats) can travel over 600 miles. Well, that's a long way away from the zoo.

So, I had a mixed experience. I loved seeing the animals, but I felt bad for some of them because they couldn't be themselves. I know, that's just me thinking I know what an animal would feel. But here's what I think: If you put me in a big apartment with everything I might need, it would be great. For a day or two. And then I would want to go and do the things I do every day and be myself. That's what this blog is all about.

What do you think about zoos? As usual, I want your comments.

20

C

30

40

---

2. ◀ **REREAD** Reread lines 3–14 of "Functions of a Zoo." Restate the reasons zoo advocates cite in support of the existence of zoos.

Animals in zoos are better cared for than in the wild, and their species can be protected. People can study the animals and their behavior. Visitors can learn more about the animals on the planet.

3. **READ** ▶ As you read lines 1–41 of "Sonia's Blog," continue to cite evidence.

- In the margin, state the topic of Sonia's blog entry.
- Circle some positive statements Sonia makes about the zoo.
- Underline some critical statements Sonia makes about the zoo.

64

---

4. ◀ **REREAD** Reread lines 1–10 of "Sonia's Blog". Explain how the zoo has changed over the years. Cite text evidence in your response.

Sonia's mother remembered "a cage with two Siberian tigers in it." However, when Sonia visits the zoo, the tigers have "a new home" that is the size of "three football fields."

65

---

2. **REREAD AND CITE TEXT EVIDENCE** Have students think about the three functions of zoos listed here.

B **ASK STUDENTS** to paraphrase the information in the second bulleted point (lines 7–10). *Students may say that animals in captivity are easier to study than animals in the wild.*

3. **READ AND CITE TEXT EVIDENCE** The blogger has positive and negative things to say about her trip to the zoo.

C **ASK STUDENTS** to think about the phrase "they seemed defeated" (line 23). What does this comment refer to? *It refers to the animals' expressions.* What effect do these words have on the reader? *They make you feel sorry for the animals.* Does this comment support or criticize zoos? *It criticizes zoos.*

4. **REREAD AND CITE TEXT EVIDENCE**

D **ASK STUDENTS** to read the blogger's comments comparing her mother's zoo experience with her own (lines 3–9). Have them make a general statement about how people's thinking about zoos has changed. *There is more humane treatment of animals now, as well as an attempt to reproduce the animals' natural habitat.*

FOR ELL STUDENTS ELL students may not have a good understanding of the measure of a mile. Explain to them that 600 miles is equivalent to 965 kilometers.

Association of Zoos and Aquariums

accredits:

guarantees
that
something
conforms to
certain rules
and standards

The Association of Zoos and Aquariums (AZA) is an organization that **accredits** zoos, mostly in North America. This means that the AZA carefully makes sure that animals in zoos have suitable living environments, live together in their natural social groups, and are well taken care of, helping the animals to follow their natural behavior.

(F)
(E)

Most well-known zoos are members of the AZA, but of the animal exhibits in the United States, fewer than 10% are accredited. Worldwide, there are more than 10,000 zoos.

Most animal
exhibits in the
U.S. and
around the
world
are not
accredited.

AZA Statistics on Accredited Zoos	
Accredited Zoos and Aquariums	221
Animals	752,000
Species	(6,000)
Threatened or Endangered Species	1,000
Annual Visitors	175 million
Annual Student Learners	12 million
Jobs Supported	142,000
Annual Contribution to U.S. Economy	$16 billion

5. **READ** ▶ As you read lines 1–9 of "Association of Zoos and Aquariums" and study the chart, continue to cite text evidence.

- Underline text that explains what the association is and the duties it carries out.
- In the margin, summarize lines 7–9.
- In the chart, circle the number of species housed in accredited zoos.

6. ◀ **REREAD** Reread lines 1–9 and study the chart. What evidence could you cite that supports the existence of zoos?

The AZA ensures that animals are comfortable in zoos. The chart
illustrates that zoos preserve endangered species and serve to
educate millions of students.

66

(G) # Innocent and Imprisoned

Robert McGuinness   **July 22**

(H)
The elephant behind the fence is bobbing her head repeatedly, a sign of "zoochosis"—distress resulting from being in a zoo. In the wild, elephants roam about 30 miles each day in large groups. But not here, and one wonders what crime she could have committed to be behind bars. That's not the way it works, though. Violent and unpredictable animals are not the kind that are exhibited in zoos. The zoo inmates are all innocent.

Of course, zoo conditions for animals have improved **vastly.** Cramped cages and incorrect diets have been replaced with open spaces and well-researched care. But it is impossible to recreate the living environment of a dolphin or a polar bear. A forty-year-long study showed that polar bears—along with lions, tigers, and cheetahs—exhibit great evidence of stress in captivity.

So why are these animals locked up? One answer to the question is conservation, but only a tiny number of zoos breed animals for conservation, and they release very few animals. During the twentieth century, there were 145 attempts to reintroduce populations into the wild, and only 16 of them were successful. The only way to **guarantee** a species' survival is to preserve them in the wild. Anyway, fewer than 15% of the animals on display are endangered. Many of the others are in zoos because of their **"charisma."** These are animals that paying customers want to see.

There's another reason for keeping animals under lock and key: research. In some cases, this may be helpful to the animal populations as a whole, but to me it seems unscientific. Information gained from studying animals in unnatural situations is only reliable about animals in unnatural situations.

10

20

vastly:
greatly

guarantee:
ensure

charisma:
charm

7. **READ** ▶ As you read lines 1–45 of "Innocent and Imprisoned," cite text evidence.

- Underline evidence in lines 14–23 that opposes the existence of zoos.
- Circle the counterargument in lines 24–28. Underline evidence that addresses this counterargument.
- In the margin, restate the claim of the editorial in your own words.

67

---

5. **READ AND CITE TEXT EVIDENCE** Have students look at lines 7–9, stating that "fewer than 10% [of all zoos] are accredited."

(E) **ASK STUDENTS** to cite two pieces of evidence that can be used to support this statement. *Students should cite line 9, "Worldwide, there are more than 10,000 zoos," as well as Accredited Zoos and Aquariums shown in the chart (221 are accredited).*

6. **REREAD AND CITE TEXT EVIDENCE**

(F) **ASK STUDENTS** what evidence they can cite that supports the idea that zoos should be better regulated. *Students may cite the fact that fewer than 10% of all zoos are accredited—which means most of them are not (lines 8–9).*

Critical Vocabulary: accredits (line 2 of "Association of Zoos and Aquariums") Have students explain the meaning of *accredits*. What inference can be made about the zoos the AZA accredits? *They have passed AZA inspections and/or demonstrated compliance with certain regulations.*

7. **READ AND CITE TEXT EVIDENCE**

(G) **ASK STUDENTS** to consider the words in the title, "innocent" and "imprisoned." What inferences can you make about the writer's argument based on the title? *The writer will probably say that zoo animals are "innocent" and shouldn't be locked up.*

Critical Vocabulary: vastly (line 8) What else can students think of that has improved *vastly* over the years? *Students may suggest computers and cell phone technology.*

Critical Vocabulary: guarantee (line 19) What does it mean when a you get a lifetime *guarantee* on a piece of merchandise? *The company will fix or replace the item if it malfunctions.*

Critical Vocabulary: charisma (line 22) Ask students to name zoo animals they think have the greatest *charisma*. *Students may name seals, chimpanzees, or dolphins.*

61

CLOSE READ
Notes

There is no zoo that serves animals, so we should take care of animals in the wild.

30 Zoos also provide their customers an education. In most cases, however, the information given about an animal is very brief and presented on a small sign that few people bother to read. People tend to talk to their friends as they watch the exotic animals, rather than learn about their particular traits and characteristics. Visitors may watch in surprise as lions choose the freezing outdoors over heated shelters, but never learn that these animals once roamed freely throughout Europe.

The final main reason for having zoos is entertainment. This is obviously unfair to the animals that are imprisoned to entertain us. There are numerous television shows and movies that show us 40 animals in their natural environments, behaving in ways that are natural to them.

A zoo that really suited animals would be a failure. It would be huge, and many of the animals would remain out of sight. The money spent supporting zoos would be better used trying to save animals in their natural surroundings, where they belong.

---

8. **◀ REREAD AND DISCUSS** Reread lines 1–45. With a small group, discuss whether you find the writer's argument convincing. Cite reasons and evidence from the text that you find are the strongest or the weakest.

SHORT RESPONSE

Cite Text Evidence What is your position on the existence of zoos? Write an argument in favor of or against zoos. **Cite text evidence** to support your claim and address any counterarguments.

Sample response: I am in favor of the existence of zoos. Zoos serve an important educational function for both students like Sonia and researchers. Zoos also protect endangered species. The AZA ensures that animals are safe and comfortable. Even people who think zoos should be abolished, like McGuinness, have to admit that "conditions for animals have improved vastly."

68

---

8. REREAD AND DISCUSS USING TEXT EVIDENCE

Ⓗ ASK STUDENTS to assign a reporter for each group to share the strong and the weak evidence. *Strong evidence: "zoochosis" (line 2); stress in captivity (line 13); only 16 of 145 attempts at reintroducing populations were successful (lines 17–19). Weak evidence: research is unscientific (lines 25–26); few people bother to read (line 31); a suitable zoo would be a failure (line 42).*

SHORT RESPONSE

Cite Text Evidence Students should:

- make an argument for or against zoos.
- cite supporting text evidence for the argument.
- address counterarguments using reason and logic.
- use persuasive techniques such as loaded language.
- choose words that have positive or negative connotations.

TO CHALLENGE STUDENTS . . .

To increase students' familiarity with different kinds of zoos, have them conduct research on zoos in their area and beyond.

ASK STUDENTS to choose a zoo to research.

- Have them use a chart similar to the one on page 66 to list facts and figures about their zoo.
- Have groups compare and contrast their zoo with the rest of the nation's zoos on a number of criteria, including how many of each kind of animal there are.
- Groups can establish their own criteria for rating zoos, such as the animals' diets, medical treatment, exercise, interaction with their peers, and how well their zoo environments replicate the conditions of home.
- Have students give their zoo a "rating."

ASK STUDENTS to conduct research on zoos around the world. Have them include information such as:

- the number of animals.
- the variety of animals.
- the number of visitors.
- the treatment of old or sick animals.

After groups have completed their research, they can work together to rate the zoos based on predetermined criteria.

DIG DEEPER

1. With the class, return to Question 3, Read. Have students share their responses.

ASK STUDENTS to review lines 35–39 of "Sonia's Blog" and analyze the analogy the writer uses comparing herself to the animals in the zoo. Have them discuss the following points:

- How is the "big apartment" like a zoo?
- How would the writer feel about living in the big apartment at first?
- How would she feel about it in the long term?
- How does she imagine the animals feel about living in a zoo?
- Students can use their answers to draw conclusions about the writer's overall feeling about zoos.

2. With the class, return to Question 8, Reread and Discuss. Have students share their responses.

ASK STUDENTS to discuss this writer's point of view about zoos.

- Have students think about the word *zoochosis*. What specific connotations does this word carry? Does the use of this term help or hinder the effectiveness of the writer's argument?
- Have students discuss how effectively the McGuinness article addresses the bulleted claims in "Functions of a Zoo" (lines 1–14). Does McGuinness provide counterarguments for each of the claims made?
- Do students agree with McGuinness? Are there flaws in his logic? Does he provide enough evidence to support his conclusions?

ASK STUDENTS to return to their Short Response answer and revise it based on the class discussion.

CLOSE READING NOTES

63

What Do Fish Have to Do with Anything?

Short Story by Avi

Why This Text

Students may have difficulty understanding why the characters in a story behave the way they do. In this story, the complex relationships between a boy, his mother, and a homeless man become clear only with an analysis of each character's motivations. Students will study the characters' reactions and determine why they behave in the ways they do as the plot moves forward. With the help of the close-reading questions, students will better understand each character's motivations and why they react to each other as they do.

Background Have students read the background information about the author. Point out that because of his lifelong dysgraphia (inability to distinguish letters), Avi often fails to see spelling errors in his work. Although he cites the discovery of the computer spellchecker as "one of the happiest moments of his life," he knows it's far from perfect, and must work doubly hard to get things right, often rewriting his work "fifty or sixty times" before he's satisfied. As students read this story, have them note that despite its apparent simplicity it represents many hours of hard work.

SETTING A PURPOSE Ask students to pay attention to the way the author uses word choice, sentence structure, dialogue, and tone to reveal character.

Common Core Support

- cite textual evidence
- describe how characters respond or change as the plot moves toward a resolution
- analyze the impact of specific word choice on meaning and tone

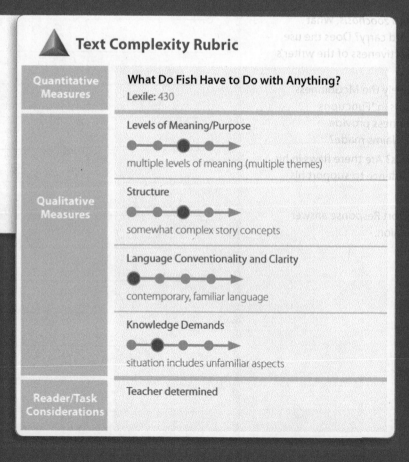

Text Complexity Rubric

Quantitative Measures

What Do Fish Have to Do with Anything?
Lexile: 430

Qualitative Measures

Levels of Meaning/Purpose

multiple levels of meaning (multiple themes)

Structure

somewhat complex story concepts

Language Conventionality and Clarity

contemporary, familiar language

Knowledge Demands

situation includes unfamiliar aspects

Reader/Task Considerations

Teacher determined

Strategies for CLOSE READING

Describe Characters' Reactions

Students should read this story carefully all the way through. Close-reading questions at the bottom of the page will help them analyze the way characters respond or change as the plot moves toward a resolution. As they read, students should jot down comments or questions about the text in the margins.

WHEN STUDENTS STRUGGLE . . .

To help students identify examples of how character is revealed in "What Do Fish Have to Do with Anything?," have them work in small groups to fill out a chart like the one below.

CITE TEXT EVIDENCE For practice in recognizing a character's motivations, have students explain what each character's actions or reactions reveal about the character.

Action or Reaction	What It Reveals
Mrs. Markham carefully cuts a half-inch piece of cake (line 39) and explains that it is a portion. (lines 45–46)	Mrs. Markham needs everything to be in order in her world.
Mrs. Markham tells Willie to do his homework rather than answering his question about her being unhappy. (lines 85–86)	Mrs. Markham doesn't want to deal with the fact that she is unhappy.
Willie gives the homeless man money. (lines 127–128)	Willie is compassionate and he wants to find out why his mother is nervous about the man.
The homeless man says he believes Willie about the cave fish. (lines 270–277)	Although he doesn't trust much, the man has judged that Willie is straightforward.

Background Avi *says he became a writer out of sheer stubbornness. In elementary school and high school, he failed many subjects, not knowing that he suffered from a serious learning disability. Still, he was determined to prove that he could write if he set his mind to it. First, Avi wrote for adults with little success. He didn't discover his true audience until he became a father and took an interest in writing for children and young adults. He has written over 70 books and received the Newbury Medal and the Newbury Honor award for his work.*

What Do Fish Have to Do with Anything?

Short Story by Avi

CLOSE READ
Notes

1. **READ ▶** As you read lines 1–23, begin to collect and cite text evidence.
   - Underline details that describe Willie's behavior.
   - In the margin, explain why Willie feels lonely.
   - Circle details that describe the man Willie sees (lines 17–23).

Every day at three o'clock Mrs. Markham waited for her son, Willie, to come out of school. They walked home together. If asked why she did it, Mrs. Markham would say, "Parents need to watch their children."

As they left the schoolyard, Mrs. Markham inevitably asked, "How was school?"

Willie would begin to talk, then stop. He was never sure his mother was listening. She seemed **preoccupied** with her own thoughts. She had been like that ever since his dad had abandoned them six months ago. No one knew where he'd gone. Willie had the feeling that his mother was lost too. It made him feel lonely.

One Monday afternoon, as they approached the apartment building where they lived, she suddenly tugged at him. "Don't look that way," she said.

Willie feels lonely because his mother has been distracted since his father left.

preoccupied: *absorbed in thought*

69

---

1. **READ AND CITE TEXT EVIDENCE** In lines 17–23, the author describes the man sitting on the milk crate.

   A ASK STUDENTS about the man's appearance. What can you infer about him from details in the text? *He is probably homeless ("His matted, streaky gray hair hung like a ragged curtain over his dirty face."); he is begging for money ("One hand was palm up.").*

   Critical Vocabulary: preoccupied (line 8) Have students explain the meaning of *preoccupied*. How does Willie's mother's preoccupation affect Willie? *It makes him think she doesn't care about him.*

"Where?"

"At that man over there."

B
A
Willie stole a look over his shoulder. A man, whom Willie had never seen before, was sitting on a red plastic milk crate near the curb. His matted, streaky gray hair hung like a ragged curtain over his
20 dirty face. His shoes were torn. Rough hands lay upon his knees. One hand was palm up. No one seemed to pay him any mind. Willie was certain he had never seen a man so utterly alone. It was as if he were some spat-out piece of chewing gum on the pavement.

"What's the matter with him?" Willie asked his mother in a hushed voice.

Keeping her eyes straight ahead, Mrs. Markham said, "He's sick." She pulled Willie around. "Don't stare. It's rude."

"What kind of sick?"

As Mrs. Markham searched for an answer, she began to walk
30 faster. "He's unhappy," she said.

"What's he doing?"

"Come on, Willie, you know perfectly well. He's begging."

"Do you think anyone gave him anything?"

"I don't know. Now, come on, don't look."

"Why don't you give him anything?"

"We have nothing to spare."

---

2. **◀ REREAD** Reread lines 1–23. What does Willie's action in line 17 reveal about his character? Support your answer with text evidence.

Willie is a curious boy who wants to learn about things he doesn't know about. He also may be a little disobedient since he disregards his mother's request not to look "that way" at the man.

---

3. **READ ▶** As you read lines 24–61, continue to cite text evidence.

- Underline the questions that Willie asks his mother in lines 24–36.
- In the margin, restate in your own words the most significant thing Mrs. Markham says in lines 49–52.
- Circle what Mrs. Markham does that reminds Willie of the homeless man.

When they got home, Mrs. Markham removed a white cardboard box from the refrigerator. It contained pound cake. Using her thumb as a measure, she carefully cut a half-inch piece of cake and gave it to
40 Willie on a clean plate. The plate lay on a plastic mat decorated with images of roses with diamondlike dewdrops. She also gave him a glass of milk and a folded napkin. She moved slowly.

Willie said, "Can I have a bigger piece of cake?"

Mrs. Markham picked up the cake box and ran a **manicured** pink fingernail along the nutrition information panel. "A half-inch piece is a portion, and a portion contains the following health requirements. Do you want to hear them?"

"No."

C
"It's on the box, so you can believe what it says. Scientists study
50 people, then write these things. If you're smart enough you could become a scientist. Like this." Mrs. Markham tapped the box. "It pays well."

Willie ate his cake and drank the milk. When he was done he took care to wipe the crumbs off his face as well as to blot his milk mustache with the napkin. His mother liked him to be neat.

His mother said, "Now go on and do your homework. Carefully. You're in sixth grade. It's important."

Willie gathered up his books that lay on the empty third chair. At the kitchen entrance he paused and looked back at his mother. She
60 was staring sadly at the cake box, but he didn't think she was seeing it. Her unhappiness made him think of the man on the street.

manicured:
trimmed and polished

You can trust what you read if it comes from a source of authority.

---

4. **◀ REREAD** Reread lines 37–52. What can you infer about Mrs. Markham based on her dialogue and the description of her behavior?

Mrs. Markham accepts things at face value. She doesn't look beneath the surface of what she reads and does not ask deep questions.

---

5. **READ ▶** As you read lines 62–88, continue to cite text evidence.

- Underline each occurrence of the word *unhappiness*.
- Circle answers that Mrs. Markham gives that do not really address Willie's questions.
- In the margin, explain the salesman's quotation in line 81.

---

2. **REREAD AND CITE TEXT EVIDENCE** Point out how the author's word choice expresses ideas. Have students look at the word *stole* in the sentence "Willie stole a look over his shoulder" (line 17).

B **ASK STUDENTS** to think about the word's connotation. Is it positive or negative? *It is negative.* Why does the author say that Willie "stole" a look? *Willie is doing something forbidden.*

3. **READ AND CITE TEXT EVIDENCE** Explain that the dialogue in lines 49–52 reveals Mrs. Markham's character.

C **ASK STUDENTS** to think about the line "It's on the box, so you can believe what it says." What do these words tell you about Mrs. Markham? *She is rigid and authoritarian; she believes in rules.*

4. **REREAD AND CITE TEXT EVIDENCE** Have students note the way Mrs. Markham measures and cuts the cake (lines 38–40).

D **ASK STUDENTS** to analyze her behavior. What does it tell you about her? *She doesn't trust her instincts.* In line 40, Mrs. Markham puts the cake on a "clean plate." Why is that detail important? *The author is emphasizing Mrs. Markham's insistence on being "proper."*

5. **READ AND CITE TEXT EVIDENCE**

E **ASK STUDENTS** what they know about Mrs. Markham that might explain her behavior. *She wants to ward off further discussion of "unhappiness"; she wants Willie to do well in school; she wants him to be successful.*

Critical Vocabulary: manicured (line 44) Have students explain the meaning of *manicured*. Ask them what Mrs. Markham's "manicured" nails say about her. *She cares about appearances.*

"What *kind* of unhappiness do you think he has?" he suddenly asked.

"Who's that?"

"That man."

Mrs. Markham looked puzzled.

"The begging man. The one on the street."

"Oh, could be anything," his mother said, **vaguely**. "A person can be unhappy for many reasons." She turned to stare out the window, as
70 if an answer might be there.

E "Is unhappiness a sickness you can cure?"

"I wish you wouldn't ask such questions."

"Why?"

F After a moment she said, "Questions that have no answers shouldn't be asked."

"Can I go out?"

"Homework first."

Willie turned to go again.

"Money," Mrs. Markham suddenly said. "Money will cure a lot of
80 unhappiness. That's why that man was begging. A salesman once said to me, 'Maybe you can't buy happiness, but you can rent a lot of it.' You should remember that."

"How much money do we have?"

"Not enough."

"Is that why you're unhappy?"

"Willie, do your homework."

Willie started to ask another question, but decided he would not get an answer. He left the kitchen.

vaguely:

with
uncertainty

The salesman
suggests that
money can at
least make
people
somewhat
happy.

6. **◀ REREAD AND DISCUSS** Reread lines 62–88. In a small group, discuss the reasons why Mrs. Markham avoids responding to Willie's questions about unhappiness.

7. **READ ▶** As you read lines 89–134, continue to cite text evidence.
   • Underline instances of Willie looking at the homeless man.
   • In the margin, describe the way the dog and Willie are similar.
   • Circle the text in which Willie disobeys his mother (lines 120–134).

72

The apartment had three rooms. The walls were painted mint
90 green. Willie walked down the hallway to his room, which was at the front of the building. By climbing up on the windowsill and pressing against the glass he could see the sidewalk five stories below. The man was still there.

It was almost five when he went to tell his mother he had finished his school assignments. He found her in her dim bedroom, sleeping. Since she had begun working the night shift at a convenience store —two weeks now—she took naps in the late afternoon.

For a while Willie stood on the **threshold**, hoping his mother would wake up. When she didn't, he went to the front room and
100 looked down on the street again. The begging man had not moved.

Willie returned to his mother's room.

"I'm going out," he announced—softly.

Willie waited a decent interval for his mother to waken. When she did not, he made sure his keys were in his pocket. Then he left the apartment.

By standing just outside the building door, he could keep his eyes on the man. It appeared as if he had still not moved. Willie wondered how anyone could go without moving for so long in the chill October air. Was staying still part of the man's sickness?

110 During the twenty minutes that Willie watched, no one who passed looked in the beggar's direction. Willie wondered if they even saw the man. Certainly no one put any money into his open hand.

G A lady leading a dog by a leash went by. The dog strained in the direction of the man sitting on the crate. His tail wagged. The lady pulled the dog away. "Heel!" she commanded.

The dog—tail between his legs—scampered to the lady's side. Even so, the dog twisted around to look back at the beggar.

Willie grinned. The dog had done exactly what Willie had done when his mother told him not to stare.

120 Pressing deep into his pocket, Willie found a nickel. It was warm
H and slippery. He wondered how much happiness you could rent for a nickel.

Squeezing the nickel between his fingers, Willie walked slowly toward the man. When he came before him, he stopped, suddenly nervous. The man, who appeared to be looking at the ground, did not move his eyes. He smelled bad.

threshold:

piece of wood
or stone
beneath a
door; doorway

Both Willie
and the dog
did the
opposite of
what they
were told and
acknowledged
the homeless
man.

73

6. **REREAD AND DISCUSS USING TEXT EVIDENCE** In lines 74–75, Mrs. Markham tells Willie, "Questions that have no answers shouldn't be asked."

F ASK STUDENTS to discuss Willie's response to this comment. What does he say? *"Can I go out?"* Why might he say that? What might be on his mind? *He might be planning to go out and see the homeless man.*

7. **READ AND CITE TEXT EVIDENCE** In lines 113–115, the lady pulls the dog away from the homeless man and gives the command "Heel!"

G ASK STUDENTS why Willie identifies with the dog. *They are both being pulled away reluctantly from the homeless man.* How is the lady like his mother? *They are both severe and controlling.*

Critical Vocabulary: vaguely (line 68) Have students share definitions. How do you feel when someone gives a "vague" answer? *Students may say they feel impatient or frustrated.*

Critical Vocabulary: threshold (line 98) Have students share definitions of *threshold*. Explain that the word is used in expressions such as "the threshold of adulthood." What does this expression mean? *It means "the start of adulthood."*

FOR ELL STUDENTS Clarify the meaning of *decent*. Explain that, as it is used in the text, it means "fairly good."

"Here." Willie stretched forward and dropped the coin into the man's open right hand.

"God bless you," the man said hoarsely as he folded his fingers
130 over the coin. His eyes, like high beams on a car, flashed up at Willie, then dropped.

Willie waited for a moment, then went back up to his room. From his window he looked down on the street. He thought he saw the coin in the man's hand, but was not sure.

After supper Mrs. Markham readied herself to go to work, then kissed Willie good night. As she did every night, she said, "If you have regular problems, call Mrs. Murphy downstairs. What's her number?"

"274-8676," Willie said.

"Extra bad problems, call Grandma."
140 "369-6754."

"Super special problems, you can call me."

"962-6743."

"Emergency, the police."

"911."

"Lay out your morning clothing."

"I will."

"Don't let anyone in the door."

"I won't."

"No television past nine."
150 "I know."

"But you can read late."

Willie has all of these phone numbers because his mother wants him to be prepared in case of an emergency.

---

8. **REREAD** Reread lines 120–134. Why does Willie give money to the homeless man, especially since his mother told him to stay away?

Willie wants to find out what made his mother nervous. Willie also feels compassion for the homeless man after seeing so many people ignore him.

9. **READ** As you read lines 135–164, continue to cite text evidence.

- In the margin, explain why Willie has all these phone numbers.
- Underline what Willie learns about the fish that live in caves.
- Circle the teacher's responses to Willie's questions.

74

"You're the one who's going to be late," Willie reminded her.

"I'm leaving," Mrs. Markham said.

After she went, Willie stood for a long while in the hallway. The empty apartment felt like a cave that lay deep below the earth. That day in school Willie's teacher had told the class about a kind of fish that lived in caves. These fish could not see. They had no eyes. The teacher had said it was living in the dark cave that made them like that.

160 Willie had raised his hand and asked, "If they want to get out of the cave, can they?"

"I suppose."

"Would their eyes come back?"

"Good question," she said, but did not give an answer.

Before he went to bed, Willie took another look out the window. In the pool of light cast by the street lamp, Willie saw the man.

On Tuesday morning when Willie went to school, the man was gone. But when he came home from school with his mother, he was there again.

170 "*Please* don't look at him," his mother whispered with some urgency.

During his snack, Willie said, "Why shouldn't I look?"

"What are you talking about?"

"That man. On the street. Begging."

"I told you. He's sick. It's better to act as if you never saw him. When people are that way they don't wish to be looked at."

---

10. **REREAD** Reread lines 154–164. What does the dialogue between Willie and his teacher reveal about Willie's character?

Willie is inquisitive and intelligent. The inability of Willie's teacher to answer his question shows that Willie often asks complicated questions that are difficult to answer.

11. **READ** As you read lines 165–217, continue to cite text evidence.

- Underline details that show Willie's father was unhappy.
- In the margin, make an inference about why Willie's mother wishes Willie would not ask about her being unhappy.
- Circle the moment in the conversation when Willie mentions the sightless fish.

75

---

8. **REREAD AND CITE TEXT EVIDENCE**

H **ASK STUDENTS** to cite text evidence suggesting one reason why Willie gives the man money. *In line 121 Willie wonders "how much happiness you could rent for a nickel," suggesting that he wants to make the man happy, if only temporarily.*

9. **READ AND CITE TEXT EVIDENCE** Have students review the teacher's response in line 164: "'Good question,' she said, but did not give an answer."

I **ASK STUDENTS** to think about another person in the story that has been unwilling to give Willie an answer. *Mrs. Markham*

10. **REREAD AND CITE TEXT EVIDENCE**

J **ASK STUDENTS** to think about Willie's questions about the fish. What does he want to know? *He wants to know if they can get out of the cave and if their eyes would come back (lines 160–16 3).* Cite text evidence suggesting that Willie feels like he's living in a cave. *Willie's "empty apartment felt like a cave" (line 155).*

11. **READ AND CITE TEXT EVIDENCE** Mrs. Markham says she doesn't want to talk about her unhappiness because it "hurts" (line 200). Willie thinks there's something she's not telling him.

K **ASK STUDENTS** what Willie wants to know. *He wants to know if his mother is ashamed.* What is Mrs. Markham's response? *She doesn't answer the question; she gets irritated.*

"Why not?"

Mrs. Markham pondered for a while. "People are ashamed of being unhappy."

180 Willie looked thoughtfully at his mother. "Are you sure he's unhappy?"

"You don't have to ask if people are unhappy. They tell you all the time."

"How?"

"The way they look."

"Is that part of the sickness?"

"Oh, Willie, I don't know. It's just the way they are."

Willie **contemplated** the half-inch slice of cake his mother had just given him. A year ago his parents seemed to be perfectly happy.

190 For Willie, the world seemed easy, full of light. Then his father lost his job. He tried to get another but could not. For long hours he sat in dark rooms. Sometimes he drank. His parents began to argue a lot. One day, his father was gone.

For two weeks his mother kept to the dark. And wept.

K Willie looked at his mother. "You're unhappy," he said. "Are *you* ashamed?"

Mrs. Markham sighed and closed her eyes. "I wish you wouldn't ask that."

"Why?"

200 "It hurts me."

"But are you ashamed?" Willie persisted. He felt it was urgent that he know. So that he could do something.

She only shook her head.

Willie said, "Do you think Dad might come back?"

She hesitated before saying, "Yes, I think so."

Willie wondered if that was what she really thought.

"Do you think Dad is unhappy?" Willie asked.

"Where do you get such questions?"

"They're in my mind."

210 "There's much in the mind that need not be paid attention to."

L "Fish who live in caves have no eyes."

"What are you talking about?"

"My teacher said it's all that darkness. The fish forget how to see. So they lose their eyes."

76

contemplate:

think about

Willie's mother doesn't want to talk about her unhappiness because it is a painful subject for her and possibly for Willie.

"I doubt she said that."

"She did."

"Willie, you have too much imagination."

M After his mother went to work, Willie gazed down onto the street. The man was there. Willie thought of going down, but he knew he

220 was not supposed to leave the building when his mother worked at night. He decided to speak to the man the next day.

That afternoon—Wednesday—Willie stood before the man. "I don't have any money," Willie said. "Can I still talk to you?"

N The man lifted his face. It was a dirty face with very tired eyes. He needed a shave.

"My mother," Willie began, "said you were unhappy. Is that true?"

"Could be," the man said.

"What are you unhappy about?"

The man's eyes narrowed as he studied Willie **intently.** He said,

230 "How come you want to know?"

Willie shrugged.

"I think you should go home, kid."

"I am home." Willie gestured toward the apartment. "I live right here. Fifth floor. Where do you live?"

"Around."

"*Are* you unhappy?" Willie persisted.

The man ran a tongue over his lips. His Adam's apple bobbed. "A man has the right to remain silent," he said, and closed his eyes.

intently:

with close attention

12. **REREAD** Reread lines 195–217. Why does Willie bring up the sightless fish during their conversation?

Willie might be connecting his mother's refusal to address her unhappiness and answer his questions with the fish who have lost their eyes. Both the fish and Mrs. Markham are failing to acknowledge certain details about their circumstances.

13. **READ** As you read lines 218–264, continue to cite text evidence.

• Underline text that describes the man's appearance and behavior.
• Circle what the homeless man says to Willie in lines 237–247.
• In the margin, explain why Willie wants to find the cure for unhappiness.

77

Critical Vocabulary: contemplate (line 188) Have students share definitions. What is the difference between *contemplating* and *thinking*? *Students may say that contemplating is a deeper level of thought.*

FOR ELL STUDENTS Explain that the verb *pondered* is similar in sound to the verb *wondered*, which means "thought about something, considered something."

12. **REREAD AND CITE TEXT EVIDENCE**

L **ASK STUDENTS** to reread the lines surrounding Willie's statement, "Fish who live in caves have no eyes" (line 211). What has his mother said about his questions? *She wonders where he gets such questions, and then says that there's a lot in the mind that needs no attention.* What does her statement have to do with fish in caves? *Willie is implying that she is living in a kind of cave.*

13. **READ AND CITE TEXT EVIDENCE**

M **ASK STUDENTS** what the dialogue in lines 218–264 reveals about Willie's character. *He is curious about the world, and he is also sincere. He believes he can find out how to help his mother.*

Critical Vocabulary: intently (line 229) After they share definitions, have pairs of students look at each other *intently.*

Willie remained standing on the pavement for a while before
240 retreating back to his apartment. Once inside he looked down from
the window. The man was still there. For a moment Willie was certain
the man was looking at the apartment building and the floor where
Willie lived.

The next day, Thursday—after dropping a nickel in the man's
palm—Willie said, "I've never seen anyone look so unhappy as you
do. So I figure you must know a lot about it."

The man took a deep breath. "Well, yeah, maybe."

Willie said, "And I need to find a cure for it."

"A *what*?"

250 "A cure for unhappiness."

The man pursed his cracked lips and blew a silent whistle. Then
he said, "Why?"

"My mother is unhappy."

"Why's that?"

"My dad went away."

"How come?"

"I think because he was unhappy. Now my mother's unhappy
too—all the time. So if I found a cure for unhappiness, it would be a
good thing, wouldn't it?"

260 "I suppose. Hey, you don't have anything to eat on you, do you?"

Willie shook his head, then said, "Would you like some cake?"

"What kind?"

"I don't know. Cake."

Willie wants to find the cure for unhappiness because his dad was unhappy when he left and his mom is unhappy now.

---

14. **◀ REREAD** Reread lines 218–264. What does the homeless man's
dialogue and behavior suggest about his character?

**The description of the homeless man conveys that his life is a painful
struggle. His dialogue suggests that he may be embarrassed or
ashamed of his situation.**

15. **READ ▶** As you read lines 265–297, continue to cite text evidence.

- Underline the reasons why the homeless man believes Willie.
- Circle Willie's "grown-up name."
- In the margin, note differences between Willie's discussion with the
  man in lines 270–283 and his conversation with his mother in lines
  211–217.

"Depends on the cake."

On Friday Willie said to the man, "I found out what kind of cake
it is."

"Yeah?"

"Pound cake. But I don't know why it's called that."

"Long as it's cake it probably don't matter."

270 Neither spoke. Then Willie said, "In school my teacher said there
are fish who live in caves and the caves are so dark the fish don't have
eyes. What do you think? Do you believe that?"

"Sure."

"You do? How come?"

"Because you said so."

"You mean, just because someone *said* it you believe it?"

"Not someone. You."

Willie was puzzled. "But, well, maybe it *isn't* true."

The man grunted. "Hey, do you believe it?"

280 Willie nodded.

"Well, you're not just anyone. You got eyes. You see. You ain't no
fish."

"Oh." Willie was pleased.

"What's your name?" the man asked.

"Willie."

"That's a boy's name. What's your grown-up name?"

"William."

"And that means another thing."

"What?"

290 "I'll take some of that cake."

Willie started. "You will?" he asked, surprised.

"Just said it, didn't I?"

Willie suddenly felt excited. It was as if the man had given him a
gift. Willie wasn't sure what it was except that it was important and he
was glad to have it. For a moment he just gazed at the man. He saw
the lines on the man's face, the way his lips curved, the small scar on
the side of his chin, the shape of his eyes, which he now saw were blue.

The man trusts what Willie says and gives direct answers to his questions. Willie's mother does not trust Willie and says he asks too many questions.

---

16. **◀ REREAD AND DISCUSS** Reread lines 270–283. In a small group,
discuss why the homeless man says Willie's "got eyes." Cite evidence
from the text to support your interpretation.

---

14. **REREAD AND CITE TEXT EVIDENCE**

Ⓝ **ASK STUDENTS** what details in the text reveal things about
the homeless man's character. *Students may point out details such
as the man's dirty face and tired eyes (line 224) and his cracked lips
(line 251). He is clearly in bad shape and is not trying to do anything
about it. His initial words—"Could be", "How come you want to
know?" (lines 227 and 230)—reveal that he feels he has no reason to
trust people.*

15. **READ AND CITE TEXT EVIDENCE** Have students think about
what the homeless man says to Willie in lines 275 and 281.

Ⓞ **ASK STUDENTS** to explain the effect these words have on
Willie. *He feels like he's being taken seriously.* What else does the
man say that makes Willie feel like he is being taken seriously? *The
homeless man asks for Willie's "grown-up name" (line 286).*

16. **REREAD AND DISCUSS USING TEXT EVIDENCE**

Ⓟ **ASK STUDENTS** to review lines 281–282. Cite the words
that Willie has been longing to hear. *Students may suggest "You're
not just anyone." Why is this important to Willie? Willie needs to feel
special, unique, and respected.*

FOR ELL STUDENTS Explain that the contraction *ain't* is
a colloquialism. Challenge a volunteer to guess what the
contraction stands for.

"I'll get the cake," Willie cried and ran back to the apartment. He snatched the box from the refrigerator as well as a knife, then hurried
300   back down to the street. "I'll cut you a piece," he said, and he opened the box.

"Hey, that don't look like a pound of cake," the man said.

Willie, alarmed, looked up.

"But like I told you, it doesn't matter."

Willie held his thumb against the cake to make sure the portion was the right size. With a poke of the knife he made a small mark for the proper width.

Just as he was about to cut, the man said, "Hold it!"

Willie looked up. "What?"

310   "What were you doing there with your thumb?"

"I was measuring the size. The right portion. A person is supposed to get only one portion."

"Where'd you learn that?"

"It says so on the box. You can see for yourself." He held out the box.

The man studied the box then handed it back to Willie. "That's just lies," he said.

"How do you know?"

"William, how can a box say how much a person needs?"

320   "But it does. The scientists say so. They measured, so they know. Then they put it there."

"Lies," the man repeated.

Willie began to feel that this man knew many things. "Well, then, how much should I cut?" he asked.

The man said, "You have to look at me, then at the cake, and then you're going to have to decide for yourself."

"Oh." Willie looked at the cake. The piece was about three inches wide. Willie looked up at the man. After a moment he cut the cake into two pieces, each an inch and a half wide. He gave one piece to the
330   man and kept the other in the box.

Willie measures a piece of cake the same way his mother does.

17. **READ** ▶ As you read lines 298–349, continue to cite text evidence.

- In the margin, explain why Willie measures the cake the way he does.
- Circle the man's advice to Willie on the amount of cake to cut.
- Underline the man's "cure for unhappiness." In the margin, explain what he means.

"God bless you," the man said as he took the piece and laid it in his left hand. He began to break off pieces with his right hand and put them in his mouth one by one. Each piece was chewed thoughtfully. Willie watched him eat.

When the man was done, he licked the crumbs on his fingers.

"Now I'll give you something," the man said.

"What?" Willie said, surprised.

"The cure for unhappiness."

"You know it?" Willie asked, eyes wide.

340   The man nodded.

"What is it?"

"It's this: What a person needs is always more than they say."

"Who's *they*?" Willie asked.

The man pointed to the cake box. "The people on the box," he said.

In his mind Willie repeated what he had been told, then he gave the man the second piece of cake.

The man took it, saying, "Good man," and he ate it.

Willie grinned.

The homeless man means that a strict measurement cannot determine what each individual needs.

18. **◀ REREAD** Reread lines 305–349. Why does Willie give the man all of the cake? In what ways does his decision indicate that he has changed as a person?

Willie gives him the cake because he understands that other people may need more than we may be led to believe. This decision indicates that Willie has learned to think for himself and recognized that every individual has his or her own needs.

17. **READ AND CITE TEXT EVIDENCE**

  Q **ASK STUDENTS** to summarize the two contrasting views on the amount of cake to cut. *Willie wants to measure it out carefully the way his mother does, on the advice of the "experts"; the man tells Willie he has to decide for himself no matter what the experts say.*

18. **REREAD AND CITE TEXT EVIDENCE** In line 344, the man responds to Willie's question with the words "The people on the box."

  R **ASK STUDENTS** what the man means by this. Who are "the people on the box"? *They are the experts his mother says know everything about how much cake a person needs.*

CLOSE READ
Notes

CLOSE READ
Notes

350   The next day was Saturday. Willie did not go to school. All morning he kept looking down from his window for the man, but it was raining and he did not appear. Willie wondered where he was, but could not imagine it.

     Willie's mother woke about noon. Willie sat with her while she ate her breakfast. "I found the cure for unhappiness," he announced.

     "Did you?" his mother said. She was reading a memo from the convenience store's owner.

     "It's 'What a person needs is always more than they say.'"

     His mother put her papers down. "That's nonsense. Where did 360 you hear that?"

     "That man."

     "What man?"

     "On the street. The one who was begging. You said he was unhappy. So I asked him."

     "Willie, I told you I didn't want you to even look at that man."

     "He's a nice man. . . ."

     "How do you know?"

     "I've talked to him."

     "When? How much?"

370   Willie shrank down. "I did, that's all."

     "Willie, I forbid you to talk to him. Do you understand me? Do you? Answer me!" She was shrill.

     "Yes," Willie said, but he'd already decided he would talk to the man one more time. He needed to explain why he could not talk to him anymore.

S **T** *Willie is going to explain why he is not allowed to talk to him.*

---

19. **READ ▶** As you read lines 350–375, continue to cite text evidence.

• Underline Willie's mother's reaction to the cure for unhappiness.
• Circle the text that tells you Willie's mother is angry with him.
• In the margin, restate the reason why Willie is going to speak to the man again.

20. **◀ REREAD** Reread lines 365–375. Why is Willie's mother so upset with him? What is Willie's reaction to her anger?

Willie's mother is upset because he disobeyed her and because she is afraid for his safety. Willie listens to her but decides he is going to see the man one more time in spite of his mother's feelings.

82

> ## What a person needs is always more than they say.

     On Sunday, however, the man was not there. Nor was he there on Monday.

     "That man is gone," Willie said to his mother as they walked home from school.

380   "I saw. I'm not blind."

     "Where do you think he went?"

     "I couldn't care less. But you might as well know, I arranged for him to be gone."

     Willie stopped short. "What do you mean?"

     "I called the police. We don't need a nuisance like that around here. Pestering kids."

     "He wasn't pestering me."

     "Of course he was."

     "How do you know?"

390   "Willie, I have eyes. I can see."

     Willie glared at his mother. "No, you can't. You're a fish. You live in a cave."

V **U** *Willie wants to be called William because he is maturing and being called by a "grown-up name" reflects that.*

---

21. **READ ▶** As you read lines 376–400, continue to cite text evidence.

• Underline details in lines 376–386 that explain what has happened to the homeless man.
• Circle the dialogue that refers to the sightless fish.
• In the margin, explain why Willie insists on being called William.

83

---

19. **READ AND CITE TEXT EVIDENCE** In line 369, Mrs. Markham asks, "When? How much?" when Willie tells her he has talked to the man.

S **ASK STUDENTS** about this remark. Why does she ask "How much?" What is she concerned about? *She wants to know how many times they have spoken; she is concerned that a homeless man has gotten too friendly with her son.*

20. **REREAD AND CITE TEXT EVIDENCE** In line 370, the author describes Willie's reaction to his mother's anger. Have students think about what Willie does and says. Have them think about the author's choice of words.

T **ASK STUDENTS** how Willie's attitude is affected by his mother's harsh words. What does he do? *He "shrank down."* What does he say? *"I did, that's all."* What is happening to Willie? *Students may say that he is withdrawing or that he no longer wants to explain himself.*

21. **READ AND CITE TEXT EVIDENCE** Have students review the last paragraphs of the story (lines 391–400), in which Willie asserts himself, calling his mother "a fish."

U **ASK STUDENTS** What else does Willie say to his mother that shows the influence of the homeless man? *Students may cite the following: "My name isn't Willie. It's William," and "What a person needs is always more than they say!" (lines 395–397).*

CLOSE READ
Notes

"Fish?" retorted Mrs. Markham. "What do fish have to do with anything? Willie, don't talk nonsense."

"My name isn't Willie. It's William. And I know how to keep from being unhappy. I do!" He was yelling now. "What a person needs is always more than they say! *Always!*"

He turned on his heel and walked back toward the school. At the corner he glanced back. His mother was following. He kept going. She
400   kept following.

---

22. REREAD Reread lines 376–400. What does the sightless fish represent to Willie? Why does he call his mother a fish? Cite explicit textual evidence in your answer.

The fish represent a willingness to be "blind" to real life. He calls his mother a fish because she refuses to listen to Willie, does not respect the homeless man as an individual, and will not confront her own unhappiness.

SHORT ANSWER

Cite Text Evidence How does Willie grow and change as the story progresses? Review the notes you took as you read and **cite text evidence** in your response.

At first Willie is a curious but timid boy. His questions to his mother about the homeless man and about her own unhappiness are not answered. Eventually, his curiosity gets the best of him and he finally speaks to the man. The conversation changes Willie's outlook on life. The homeless man speaks to him as an adult and gives him the "cure for unhappiness" which is "What a person needs is always more than they say." The encounter teaches Willie the importance of thinking for himself. The final scene in which he calls his mother a "fish" and insists on being called "William" reveals that Willie has matured and learned to think for himself and to respect individuals.

84

---

22. REREAD AND CITE TEXT EVIDENCE

V **ASK STUDENTS** why Willie was angry at his mother. *She had sent the police to remove the homeless man and thought that she knew better than Willie.* What did Willie think of her actions? *He thought she couldn't see what was really happening.*

SHORT RESPONSE

Cite Text Evidence Students should:

- explain how the author develops characters and how they respond and change during the course of the story.
- interpret characters through their words and actions.
- analyze characters' motivations.
- examine the techniques the author uses to create realistic characters and dialogue.

TO CHALLENGE STUDENTS . . .

Tell students that Avi, the author of this story, is skilled at creating realistic dialogue for his characters. Giving each character his or her own voice enables readers to go beyond the literal meanings of the words and into the characters' minds. Explain that sometimes the meaning of dialogue lies more in what is not said than what is said. Some writers find it helpful to "act out" the dialogue first, to get a sense of what the character might really say in a particular situation.

ASK STUDENTS to work with a partner or small group to write new dialogue for this story. Have them invent exchanges between Willie, Mrs. Markham, and/or the homeless man in any combination. (They may even want to invent a conversation involving all three characters!) They can create a new scene, or add dialogue to a scene that exists. After they have written their dialogue, have them read it aloud to the class.

DIG DEEPER

With the class, return to Question 17, Read. Have students share their responses.

ASK STUDENTS to think about the way the author uses the simple act of cutting a cake to reveal character.

- Have students describe the cake-cutting methods used by Mrs. Markham and the homeless man.
- Have students make an inference about Mrs. Markham's insistence on measuring each slice. What might explain her inflexibility?
- Have students draw conclusions about the life of the homeless man based on his ideas about cake cutting.
- Have students contrast the way Willie cuts the cake at the beginning and at the end of the story. How does the homeless man's idea about giving people more than they ask for help Willie to become his own person?
- Students may include text evidence that shows how the homeless man's ideas challenged Willie's beliefs about himself, his mother, homeless people, blind adherence to authority, and virtually everything he'd been taught previously.

ASK STUDENTS to return to their Short Response answer and revise it based on the class discussion.

Decisions That Matter

Decisions That Matter

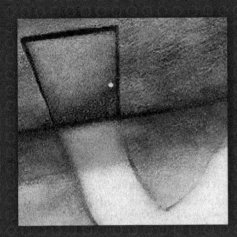

"We must never forget that it is through our actions, words, and thoughts that we have a choice."

—Sogyal Rinpoche

Community Hero: Chief Wilma Mankiller

Biography by Susannah Abbey

from Every Day Is a New Day

Autobiography by Wilma Mankiller

Why These Texts

Readers of an autobiography and a biography about the same subject may be surprised at how different the two works are. The authors not only have different points of view but also write with different purposes, and so will focus on different aspects of the subject's life. With the help of the close-reading questions, students will analyze how the biography and autobiography portray the life of Wilma Mankiller. This close reading will lead students to compare and contrast the two works.

Background Have students read the background information about Wilma Mankiller. Introduce the selection by reminding students that as the United States pushed its frontier westward during the nineteenth century, Native Americans were displaced. The U.S. government signed hundreds of treaties with conquered tribes, relocating them to reservations. The Cherokee people were forced from their homeland in the southeast to the territory of Oklahoma.

SETTING A PURPOSE Ask students to pay attention to how the two works present elements of Mankiller's personal story. How are the presentations alike and different?

Common Core Support

- cite textual evidence
- determine a central idea and summarize it
- analyze how an individual is introduced, illustrated, and elaborated
- determine an author's point of view
- compare and contrast an autobiography and a biography

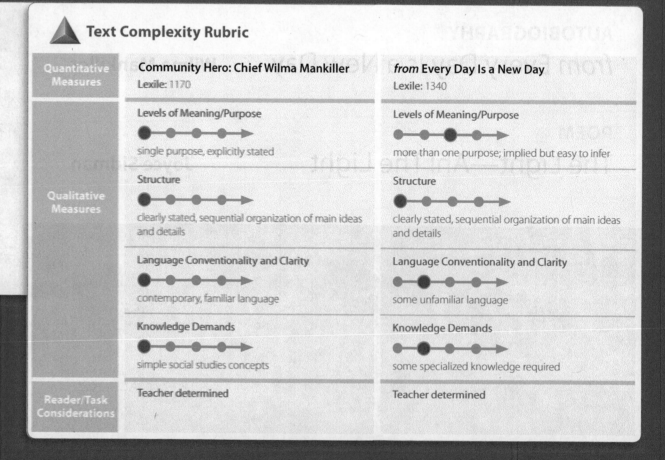

Text Complexity Rubric

	Community Hero: Chief Wilma Mankiller Lexile: 1170	*from* Every Day Is a New Day Lexile: 1340
Quantitative Measures		
Qualitative Measures	**Levels of Meaning/Purpose** single purpose, explicitly stated	**Levels of Meaning/Purpose** more than one purpose; implied but easy to infer
	Structure clearly stated, sequential organization of main ideas and details	**Structure** clearly stated, sequential organization of main ideas and details
	Language Conventionality and Clarity contemporary, familiar language	**Language Conventionality and Clarity** some unfamiliar language
	Knowledge Demands simple social studies concepts	**Knowledge Demands** some specialized knowledge required
Reader/Task Considerations	Teacher determined	Teacher determined

Strategies for CLOSE READING

Compare and Contrast: Biography and Autobiography

Students should read both works carefully all the way through. Close-reading questions at the bottom of the page will help them focus on a thorough analysis of how Mankiller is presented. As they read, students should jot down comments or questions about the text in the margins.

WHEN STUDENTS STRUGGLE . . .

To help students compare and contrast the biography and autobiography, have them work in small groups to fill out a chart like the one shown below.

CITE TEXT EVIDENCE For practice in comparing and contrasting the biography and autobiography, ask students to cite text evidence for each cell of the chart.

Biography	Autobiography
Author's Purpose	*Author's Purpose*
To explain how a girl from a poor family in Oklahoma became a Cherokee leader	*To explain why her years in the San Francisco Bay Area were important to her*
Presentation of an Event	*Presentation of an Event*
She got involved with the San Francisco Indian Center.	*She joined the occupation of Alcatraz Island in 1969.*
Here she became politicized and reinforced her identity as a Cherokee.	*That morning . . . "my heart and mind made a quantum leap forward." (lines 7–8)*
Impression of Mankiller	*Impression of Mankiller*
"She was, in truth, a natural leader." (line 49)	*"I learned that sovereignty was more than a legal concept. . . It means freedom and responsibility." (lines 65–68)*
She "continues to be a political, cultural, and spiritual leader. . . ." (line 74)	

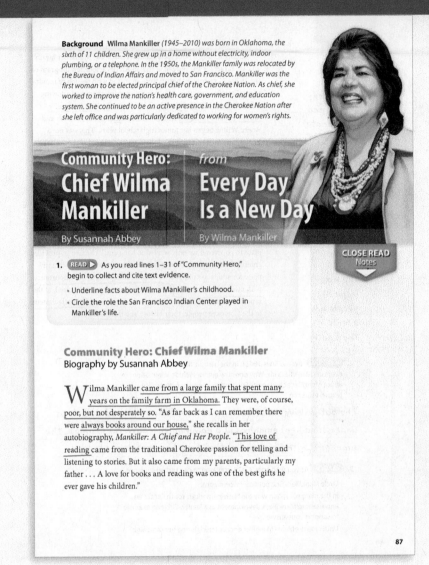

Background Wilma Mankiller *(1945–2010) was born in Oklahoma, the sixth of 11 children. She grew up in a home without electricity, indoor plumbing, or a telephone. In the 1950s, the Mankiller family was relocated by the Bureau of Indian Affairs and moved to San Francisco. Mankiller was the first woman to be elected principal chief of the Cherokee Nation. As chief, she worked to improve the nation's health care, government, and education system. She continued to be an active presence in the Cherokee Nation after she left office and was particularly dedicated to working for women's rights.*

Community Hero: **Chief Wilma Mankiller**
By Susannah Abbey

from **Every Day Is a New Day**
By Wilma Mankiller

CLOSE READ Notes

1. **READ ▷** As you read lines 1–31 of "Community Hero," begin to collect and cite text evidence.

   • Underline facts about Wilma Mankiller's childhood.
   • Circle the role the San Francisco Indian Center played in Mankiller's life.

Community Hero: Chief Wilma Mankiller
Biography by Susannah Abbey

W ilma Mankiller came from a large family that spent many years on the family farm in Oklahoma. They were, of course, poor, but not desperately so. "As far back as I can remember there were always books around our house," she recalls in her autobiography, *Mankiller: A Chief and Her People*. "This love of reading came from the traditional Cherokee passion for telling and listening to stories. But it also came from my parents, particularly my father . . . A love for books and reading was one of the best gifts he ever gave his children."

87

1. **READ AND CITE TEXT EVIDENCE** Tell students that biographies often begin with the subject's childhood. Here the biographer looks for clues about Mankiller's future in her early years as a member of a large, poor farming family in Oklahoma.

   Ⓐ **ASK STUDENTS** to discuss how they can distinguish facts from opinions in these lines. *Students should understand that facts are events or situations that occurred, so they can be supported by the historical record. For example, Mankiller returned to the Bay Area after spending a year at a family ranch and then got involved with the San Francisco Indian Center. An opinion is someone's view or appraisal of something. For example, Mankiller recalls that the Center was "a safe place to go, even if we only wanted to hang out." Point out that the distinction may be subtle. Have students explain why "This was not a happy time for her" (lines 16–17) is a fact. It describes an emotional state that Mankiller experienced; it can be verified by talking to her and to people who knew her then.*

CLOSE READ Notes

10   Unfortunately, a poor local economy made the Mankiller family an easy target for the Bureau of Indian Affairs relocation program of the 1950s. Government agents were entrusted with the job of moving rural Cherokees to cities, effectively dispersing them and allowing others to buy their traditional, oil-rich lands. In 1959 the family moved to San Francisco, where Wilma's father could get a job and where Wilma began her junior high school years. This was not a happy time for her. She missed the farm and she hated the school where white kids teased her about being Native American and about her name.

20   Mankiller decided to leave her parents and go to live with her maternal grandmother, Pearl Sitton, on a family ranch inland from San Francisco. The year she spent there restored her confidence and after returning to the Bay Area, she got increasingly involved with the world of the San Francisco Indian Center.

"There was something at the Center for everyone. It was a safe place to go, even if we only wanted to hang out." The Center provided entertainment, social and cultural activities for youth, as well as a place for adults to hold powwows and discuss matters of importance with other BIA relocatees. Here, Mankiller became politicized, at the 30   same time reinforcing her identity as a Cherokee and her attachments to the Cherokee people, their history and traditions.

Notes (left margin, handwritten):

1. The family was forced to relocate to San Francisco.

2. She left her family to live on her grandmother's ranch.

3. She was inspired by people and events at the Center.

---

2. ◀ REREAD Reread lines 10–31. In the margin, list three important events in Mankiller's life. Why does the author include information about Mankiller's childhood? Support your answer with explicit textual evidence.

The author gives information on Mankiller's childhood to help us understand her beginnings as a community leader. For example, the time spent with her grandmother gave her confidence to lead.

3. READ ▶ As you read lines 32–79, continue to cite textual evidence.

- Circle Mankiller's first political involvement.
- In the margin, explain why the Native American Youth Center was important to Mankiller's development as a leader. Circle an example to support your answer.
- Underline problems Mankiller encountered during her campaign.

88

CLOSE READ Notes

> **Mankiller says she learned on the job. . . . But she was, in truth, a natural leader.**

When a group of Native Americans occupied Alcatraz Island in November 1969, in protest of U.S. Government policies, which had, for hundreds of years, deprived them of their lands, Mankiller participated in her first major political action.

"It changed me forever," she wrote. "It was on Alcatraz . . . where at long last some Native Americans, including me, truly began to regain our balance."

In the years that followed the "occupation," Mankiller became
40   more active in developing the cultural resources of the Native American community. She helped build a school and an Indian Adult Education Center. She directed the Native American Youth Center in East Oakland, coordinating field trips to tribal functions, hosting music concerts, and giving kids a place to do their homework or just connect with each other. The youth center also gave her the opportunity to pull together Native American adults from around Oakland as volunteers, thus strengthening their ties. Mankiller says she learned on the job, joking "my enthusiasm seemed to make up for my lack of skills." But she was, in truth, a natural leader.

50   She returned to Oklahoma in the 1970s where she worked at the Urban Indian Resource Center and volunteered in the community. In 1981 she founded and then became director of the Cherokee Community Development Department, where she orchestrated a community-based **renovation** of the water system and was instrumental in lifting an entire town, Bell, Oklahoma, out of squalor and despair. In 1983, she ran for Deputy Chief of the Cherokee Nation.

Notes (right margin, handwritten):
Her early organizing experiences and community work prepared her for leadership.

renovation: *upgrade; restoration*

89

---

2. REREAD AND CITE TEXT EVIDENCE

B ASK STUDENTS why certain childhood events were important. Have them cite text evidence to support their reasoning. *Students should recognize that some events were important because they had lasting effects on Mankiller, helping her become a leader of the Cherokee people. Students could mention, for example, that getting involved with the San Francisco Indian Center was important because it led to her becoming politicized, while reinforcing her identity as a Cherokee (lines 29–31).*

3. READ AND CITE TEXT EVIDENCE

C ASK STUDENTS to paraphrase Mankiller's responsibilities at the Native American Youth Center. *She was the director. She coordinated field trips. She hosted music concerts. She gave kids a place to do their homework and connect with each other. She recruited Native American adults as volunteers.* Have students explain how these duties helped Mankiller become a leader.

Critical Vocabulary: renovation (line 54) Have students share their definitions of *renovation*. If the water system was in need of renovation, what can we say about its condition? *The water system was old or had fallen into disrepair; it wasn't being maintained in good condition.*

FOR ELL STUDENTS Clarify that the noun *squalor* means "a filthy and wretched condition."

CLOSE READ Notes

The campaign was not an easy one. There had never been a woman leader of a Native American tribe. She had many ideas to
60 present and debate, but encountered discouraging opposition from men who refused to talk about anything but the fact that she was a woman. Her campaign days were troubled by death threats, and her tires were slashed. She sought the advice of friends for ways to approach the constant insults, finally settling on a philosophy summed up by the epithet, "Don't ever argue with a fool, because someone walking by and observing you can't tell which one is the fool." In the end, Mankiller had her day: she was elected as first woman Deputy Chief, and over time her wise, strong leadership **vindicated** her supporters and proved her detractors wrong.
70 In 1985, when Chief Ross Swimmer left for Washington, D.C., Mankiller was **obligated** to step into his position, becoming the first woman to serve as Principal Chief of the Cherokee Nation. Although poor health forced her to retire from that position in 1995, Wilma Mankiller continues to be a political, cultural, and spiritual leader in her community and throughout the United States. In 1990 Oklahoma State University honored her with the Henry G. Bennett Distinguished Service Award, and in 1998, President Clinton awarded her the Presidential Medal of Freedom, the nation's highest civilian honor.

vindicate:
justify

obligate:
require

4. ◀ **REREAD AND DISCUSS** Reread lines 58–69. In a small group, discuss the possible reasons that men may have opposed having a woman as Chief. What experiences qualified Mankiller for the job? Be sure to cite evidence from the text in your discussion.

90

---

5. **READ** ▶ As you read lines 1–41 from "Every Day Is a New Day," begin to collect and cite text evidence.

- In the margin, make an inference about how Mankiller feels about her surroundings, and underline descriptive language that supports your inference.
- In the margin, summarize the indigenous people's historical connection to Alcatraz.

from Every Day Is a New Day
Autobiography by Wilma Mankiller

Though I have lived most of my life on my grandfather's Cherokee land allotment in rural Adair County, Oklahoma, I learned a great deal about **indigenous** people, governance, and land during the twenty years I spent in the San Francisco Bay Area. Soon after my Native American brothers and sisters joined the occupation of Alcatraz Island in late 1969, I made plans to visit the island. The morning I made the short journey to Alcatraz, my heart and mind made a quantum leap forward.
10 Lady dawn descended on the nearly empty streets of Fisherman's Wharf, bearing the gift of a brand-new day. Fishing boats rocked in their slips, awaiting the day's journey, as shop owners sleepily prepared for the onslaught of tourists. An occasional foghorn or the barking of a stray dog was the only sound other than the steady lap of the ocean against the docks. Alcatraz Island, several miles across San Francisco Bay, was barely visible as I boarded a boat for the former military and federal prison, which had recently been taken over by indigenous people and declared "Indian Land." Mist and fog gave the island a dreamlike quality that seemed fitting for a place where the American dream was rejected and an Indigenous dream declared.
20 The young students who occupied Alcatraz Island claimed that federal surplus lands such as Alcatraz should be returned to tribal peoples on legal and moral ground, and that treaties, land rights, and tribal **sovereignty** should be respected and honored. This was not the first relationship between indigenous people and Alcatraz. Long before Europeans arrived, Ohlones and other indigenous people of

indigenous:
original

Mankiller's surroundings are important to her. Her poetic descriptions of natural details show how much the area means to her.

sovereignty:
self-rule; independence

91

---

4. **REREAD AND DISCUSS USING TEXT EVIDENCE**

D **ASK STUDENTS** to infer why the men were against Mankiller's campaign for Deputy Chief. Have students from each group share their reasoning. *The men wouldn't talk about the issues; they just focused on the fact that Mankiller was a woman. Her friends advised Mankiller, "Don't ever argue with a fool." And there hadn't been any women leaders of Native American tribes before. All of these reasons make it seem like the men were just prejudiced against women.*

Critical Vocabulary: vindicate (line 69) Have students share their definitions of *vindicate*, and ask volunteers to use the verb in sentences.

Critical Vocabulary: obligate (line 71) Have students suggest synonyms of *obligate* that would work in this context. *bind, force, oblige*

5. **READ AND CITE TEXT EVIDENCE**

E **ASK STUDENTS** how Mankiller alerts the reader that indigenous peoples have historical connections with Alcatraz. She writes that the 1969 occupation of the island was "not the first relationship" indigenous people had with Alcatraz (lines 23–24). What were the earlier relationships? *The Ohlone and other coastal peoples used to rest on the island. The Modocs were imprisoned on the island after losing their homeland.*

Critical Vocabulary: indigenous (line 3) Have students share their definitions of *indigenous*. What distinguishes indigenous people from everyone else? *The ancestors of indigenous people originated here in the Americas; the ancestors of everyone else originated on other continents.*

Critical Vocabulary: sovereignty (line 23) Have students share their definitions of *sovereignty*, and ask volunteers to use the noun in sentences.

CLOSE READ
Notes

Alcatraz Island

At first, native peoples visited Alcatraz. For a while, it was a prison for tribal peoples. One hundred years later, American Indians occupied the island.

the coast rested and got their bearings on Alcatraz Island, called the Island of the Pelicans (Isla de los Alcatraces) after the seabirds that gathered there. In the late nineteenth century, Modocs and other tribal people were imprisoned at Alcatraz for fighting the United
30   States Army in a desperate attempt to retain their ancestral homelands. When the Spanish first settled in the mid-1700s on the land that is today California, there were more than 275,000 indigenous people living there. That changed very quickly. By 1900, fewer than 16,000 indigenous people remained. It is a miracle that even that many survived. Indigenous people of California endured widespread violence, starvation, disease, genocide, rape, and slavery. As late as 1870, a few communities in California were still paying bounties for Indian scalps or severed heads. One hundred years later, the descendants of some of the indigenous people who survived the
40   conquerors, miners, and settlers joined others at Alcatraz to find their bearings just as their ancestors had done so long ago.

6.   **REREAD AND DISCUSS** Reread lines 20–41. In a small group, explain why Alcatraz Island holds such importance for Mankiller.

7.   **READ** As you read lines 42–87, continue to cite textual evidence.

• Underline sentences that explain what Alcatraz symbolized for younger American Indians.

• Circle two pieces of information that Mankiller learns about sovereignty.

92

I visited Alcatraz several times during the nineteen-month occupation of the island. At any given time, the Alcatraz community was composed of an **eclectic** group of indigenous people, activists, civil rights veterans, students, and people who just wanted to be at a "happening." Richard Oakes, a visionary young Mohawk who emerged as an early spokesman for the Alcatraz occupiers, said,
(G) "There are many old prophecies that speak of the younger people rising up and finding a way for the People to live." (In their own
50   languages, many tribes call themselves by words that mean "the People.") Alcatraz was a catalyst for many young people who would spend their lives forging a new path for the People.

(H) The Alcatraz experience was certainly a **watershed** for me. The leaders articulated principles and ideas I had thought about but could not name or articulate. During the Alcatraz occupation and that period of activism, anything seemed possible. Inspired by Alcatraz, I began a four-year association with the Pit River Tribe, which was involved in a legal and political struggle to regain their ancestral lands near Mount Shasta. Mostly I worked as a volunteer at the tribe's
60   legal offices in San Francisco, but I frequently visited Pit River lands, where I learned about the history of indigenous people in California from traditional leaders. Occasionally one of the leaders would bring out an old cardboard box filled with tribal documents supporting their land claims. They treated the precious documents almost as sacred objects. At Pit River, I learned that sovereignty was more than a legal concept. It represents the ability of the People to articulate their own vision of the future, control their destiny, and watch over their lands. It means freedom and responsibility.

Another place that had a great impact on me was the Oakland
70   Intertribal Friendship House, which served as an oasis for a diverse group of indigenous people living in a busy urban area far from their home communities. We gathered there for dinners, meetings, and to listen to a wonderful array of speakers, including Tom Porter, a Mohawk leader who spoke about his people's fight to remain separate

CLOSE READ
Notes

eclectic:
assorted; diverse

watershed:
turning point

93

---

6.   **REREAD AND DISCUSS USING TEXT EVIDENCE**

(F) ASK STUDENTS to describe the connection Mankiller feels to the island. *Students should note that Mankiller feels connected to Alcatraz because the island is itself connected to the history of indigenous peoples, a history that is painful but vitally important to her.*

7.   **READ AND CITE TEXT EVIDENCE**

(G) ASK STUDENTS to describe what Alcatraz meant to the occupiers. How did young Native Americans' experience on Alcatraz change them? *For some, Alcatraz was the fulfillment of an old prophecy that young people would rise up and find a way for indigenous people to live. For others, Alcatraz was a catalyst, something that made them spend the rest of their lives searching for a better path. And for Mankiller, it was a watershed, a moment when she realized important principles and decided to become an activist.*

Critical Vocabulary: eclectic (line 44) Have students share their definitions of *eclectic*. Why does Mankiller describe the group of Alcatraz occupiers as eclectic? *The group was eclectic because it was made up of different kinds of people.*

Critical Vocabulary: watershed (line 53) Have students share their definitions of *watershed*. What makes Alcatraz a watershed for Mankiller? *The Alcatraz experience was a watershed because it marked a turning point in her life.*

FOR ELL STUDENTS Clarify that in this context a catalyst is an event that causes a change or an action; in chemistry it means a substance that causes a change or an action.

CLOSE READ
Notes

and independent. He explained that the Mohawk's 1795 treaty with the United States provided that they had the "perpetual right to live on their reservations in independent sovereignty, never to be disturbed." He spoke movingly about the important role women play among his people. He said that traditional Iroquois women selected

80 the chiefs and could **depose** them if they did not perform their duties properly. The speech had a powerful, lasting impact on me.

My experiences at Alcatraz and Pit River led me to cofound, with Joe Carillo, California Indians for a Fair Settlement, which encouraged California tribal people to reject a proposed settlement of all land claims for only pennies per acre. All this work helped me to understand more fully the historical context in which tribal people live our contemporary lives.

In 1976 I was further **galvanized** by a treaty conference at the Standing Rock Sioux Reservation in Wakpala, South Dakota, that

90 readied delegates for the 1977 United Nations Conference on

depose:
overthrow; remove

galvanize:
excite; inspire

> ## " All peoples have the right to self-determination. "

Indigenous Rights in Geneva. I had been working as a volunteer to help indigenous people prepare for the Geneva conference by documenting the fact that from the time of initial contact with Europeans, tribal communities were treated as separate nations, and numerous agreements between the emerging United States and tribal nations were signed.

At Wakpala, tribal sovereignty was framed as an issue of international significance. The concept of self-determination in international law as defined by UN General Assembly Resolution 1514

100 resonates with indigenous people: "All peoples have the right to self-determination. By virtue of that right they freely determine their political status and freely pursue their economic, social, and cultural development."

During this time, I also came to understand that among some tribal people, including the Cherokee, there was a historical period when there was little separation between political and spiritual organizations. Cherokee spiritual leaders were involved in conducting the council meetings that provided some of the political structure whereby major decisions were made by the entire settlement. Council

110 meetings were often held after or during ceremonies, which helped prepare the people to deal with major issues affecting the community. However, in contemporary times, there is a formal separation between the political organization and spiritual practitioners.

---

8. **REREAD** Reread lines 53–87. Summarize what Mankiller learns from her work at Alcatraz, with the Pit River Tribe, and in Oakland. What did her experiences teach her? Support your answer with explicit textual evidence.

Mankiller's work with various tribal leaders at these places taught her to "articulate principles and ideas" she had never been able to voice. She learned that sovereignty meant "freedom and responsibility." Her experiences at Alcatraz and Pit River inspired her to cofound an organization that united tribal people throughout California.

9. **READ** As you read lines 88–116, continue to cite textual evidence.

- Underline the relationship between political and spiritual organizations in the present and in the past.
- Circle what Mankiller thought of her experiences with the tribes.

94

95

---

8. **REREAD AND CITE TEXT EVIDENCE**

H ASK STUDENTS to find and cite examples of lessons that Mankiller learned at the three locations. *Students should note that she learned to articulate principles and ideas (line 54), a fuller concept of sovereignty (lines 65–68), and the importance of women's role in indigenous society (lines 78–81).*

9. **READ AND CITE TEXT EVIDENCE**

I ASK STUDENTS to find and paraphrase what Mankiller learned about political and spiritual organizations. *She learned that historically there wasn't much separation between the two kinds of organizations (lines 104–109).*

Critical Vocabulary: depose (line 80) Have students share their definitions of *depose,* and ask volunteers to use the verb in sentences.

Critical Vocabulary: galvanize (line 88) Have students suggest synonyms of the verb *galvanize* that would work in this context. *energize, motivate, spur*

FOR ELL STUDENTS Some students may be familiar with the expression *to be framed* as meaning "to be set up." Explain that the meaning of the phrase *was framed* in this context is "was planned."

CLOSE READ
Notes

The Alcatraz, Pit River, California Indian for a Fair Settlement, and the treaty Conference experiences were great preparation for my future role as principal chief of the Cherokee Nation.

10. ◀ **REREAD AND DISCUSS** Reread lines 97–103. Work with a small group to paraphrase the concept of self-determination as stated by UN General Assembly Resolution 1514. Why did this resolution mean so much to Mankiller? Cite explicit text evidence in your discussion.

SHORT RESPONSE

Cite Text Evidence In what ways is Wilma Mankiller's autobiographical account of her life different from Susannah Abbey's biography? Compare and contrast the information presented in each text. Review your reading notes for both texts, and be sure to **cite text evidence** in your response.

Mankiller focuses on her time at Alcatraz and on specific experiences that influenced the development of her thoughts and actions. Mankiller spends less time on her early life, while Abbey provides more background on Mankiller's childhood—such as her time in junior high school, which was "not a happy time for her." Mankiller does not discuss her leadership abilities, but provides details about how her experiences shaped and inspired her, especially through her association with people like Richard Oakes, Tom Porter, and Joe Carillo. Abbey writes that Mankiller is "a natural leader" with "wise, strong leadership." Mankiller writes about the history of indigenous people, while Abbey writes only about Mankiller. Mankiller expresses her feelings about her life, while Abbey uses quotes from Mankiller's autobiography and includes her own opinions of Mankiller's character.

96

---

10. REREAD AND DISCUSS USING TEXT EVIDENCE

🟡 **ASK STUDENTS** in each group to choose a volunteer to read the group's paraphrase of Resolution 1514. Have students find and discuss earlier instances in which Mankiller examines the issue of sovereignty. *The people who occupied Alcatraz Island fought for tribal sovereignty (lines 20–24), tribal elders at the Pit River taught Mankiller the full meaning of sovereignty (lines 65–68), and Tom Porter spoke movingly about the Mohawks' long struggle for sovereignty (lines 73–78). Resolution 1514 resonated with Mankiller because it was something she'd been thinking about most of her life.*

SHORT RESPONSE

Cite Text Evidence Students should:

- describe parts of Mankiller's life presented by each text.
- describe qualities of Mankiller emphasized by each text.
- give examples of differences between the texts.

TO CHALLENGE STUDENTS . . .

For deeper understanding, students can research the political and social context of the 1969 occupation of Alcatraz Island.

ASK STUDENTS what events led up to the occupation. *Students should understand that the 1960s were years of social unrest and civic protest in the United States. Ever greater numbers of U.S. troops were being sent to fight in Vietnam—a war that many Americans came to question. By the end of the decade, protests against the war were being staged on college campuses across the country. At the same time, Cesar Chavez was organizing Mexican and Chicano farm workers in California. The aim was to form a union that could increase the wages and improve living conditions for a group that had been marginalized for centuries. The 1960s were also crucial years in the civil rights movement, led by African Americans such as Martin Luther King Jr. and Malcolm X. Their efforts would eventually change the social and legal foundations of the country.*

At the time, living standards of Native Americans were among the worst in the country. Politically and economically oppressed, isolated on reservations, indigenous peoples lived in poverty. Observing the various movements of social protest in the 1960s, young Native Americans decided to take their own stand—the occupation of Alcatraz Island.

DIG DEEPER

1. With the class, return to Question 4, Reread and Discuss. Have students share the results of their discussion.

ASK STUDENTS to share the main conclusions of their group discussions.

- What kind of evidence did the groups cite for the men's opposition to Mankiller's candidacy? *Students should note that the men didn't seem to oppose Mankiller on substantive issues or differences of opinion about tribal policy. And some of the opposition was extreme, even illegal. The author records that Mankiller received death threats and had her tires slashed (lines 63–64).*

- Have groups discuss and evaluate the inferences they drew about the men's opposition. *Students will probably support their inferences that the men were prejudiced against women—especially in important roles—from the details that the author presents. The men's constant insults and refusal to engage Mankiller seriously are convincing evidence.*

- Ask students to summarize their group's conclusions about Mankiller's qualifications for the job. How did her life experiences give her skills she would need to be Deputy Chief? *Students should talk about her involvement with the San Francisco Indian Center, her participation in the Alcatraz occupation, her work at the Native American Youth Center, and her experience directing the Cherokee Community Development Department.*

2. With the class, return to Question 6, Reread and Discuss. Have students share the results of their discussion.

ASK STUDENTS to compare Alcatraz Island with its occupiers.

- What similarities did Mankiller see in the island and the young Native Americans who occupied it? *The occupiers, writes Mankiller, were the descendants of the small group of indigenous people who survived the violence and disease of European conquest. The island, declared "Indian Land" by the occupiers, was a tiny piece of California, which once belonged to their ancestors. Both were remnants of what were once greater wholes.*

ASK STUDENTS to return to their Short Response answer and revise it based on the class discussion.

CLOSE READING NOTES

The Light—Ah! The Light

Poem by Joyce Sidman

Why This Text

Students need practice analyzing the structure of narrative poetry. Narrative poetry shares many features with the short story, such as characters, setting, and plot. With the help of the close-reading questions, students will analyze the narrative structure of "The Light—Ah! The Light." This close reading will lead students to an analysis of Marie Curie's character as she is presented in the poem.

Background Have students read the background and the information about the author. Introduce the selection by telling students that Marie Curie did well in school. In 1883, however, she could not go to college in Poland because she was a woman. That did not stop her. First she attended a secret school called the Flying University. Then she moved to France and studied at the University of Paris. She discovered polonium and radium and won the Nobel Prize twice!

SETTING A PURPOSE Ask students to pay attention to details such as characters, setting, and plot. What is the first thing you learn about Marie Curie?

Common Core Support

- cite textual evidence
- determine the meaning of words and phrases as they are used in a text
- analyze how a line or stanza fits into the overall structure of a text
- analyze how a line or stanza contributes to the development of the setting or plot

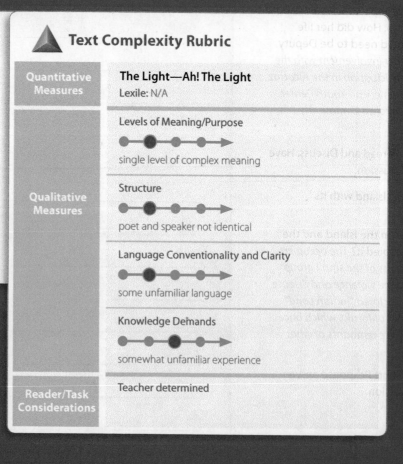

Text Complexity Rubric

The Light—Ah! The Light
Lexile: N/A

Quantitative Measures

Qualitative Measures

Levels of Meaning/Purpose
single level of complex meaning

Structure
poet and speaker not identical

Language Conventionality and Clarity
some unfamiliar language

Knowledge Demands
somewhat unfamiliar experience

Reader/Task Considerations
Teacher determined

Analyze Structure: Narrative Poetry

Students should read the poem carefully all the way through. Close-reading questions at the bottom of the page will help them focus on a thorough analysis of the text. As they read, students should jot down comments or questions about the poem in the side margins.

WHEN STUDENTS STRUGGLE . . .

To help students determine the narrative elements of the poem, have them work in small groups to fill out a chart like the ones shown as they analyze the text.

CITE TEXT EVIDENCE For practice in analyzing narrative elements such as character, setting, and plot, ask students to cite details from the poem.

Element	Questions to Ask and Answer
Characters	**Who is the main character?** *Marie Curie*
	What is the main character like? *defiant: "spit at the obelisk erected by the Tsar" determined: "Poverty, prejudice . . .I swept aside."*
Setting	**What information or clues tell you where and when the story takes place?** *"in Warsaw under . . . Russian rule" "Paris."*
	How is the setting important to the poem? *Curie moved from Warsaw, Poland, to Paris, France, to study at "the Sorbonne."*
Plot	**What central conflict or struggle does the main character face?** *"The work was brutal"; it "ravaged my skin, poisoned my blood"*
	How is the conflict resolved? *Curie is satisfied by what she has accomplished in her life, despite the costs to her health.*

Background *Born in 1956,* **Joyce Sidman** *is an award-winning American writer known for her inventive poetry. Her poem, "The Light—Ah! The Light" takes as its subject the physicist and chemist Marie Curie. Born Marie Skłodowska in Warsaw, Poland, in 1867, Marie Curie studied at the University of Paris (referred in the poem as the Sorbonne) and discovered the chemical elements polonium and radium. She is best known for discovering the principles of radioactivity, which refers to the loss of particles and energy from certain atomic elements. Sidman reimagines Curie's thoughts and feelings in the poem.*

The Light—Ah! The Light
(Marie Curie discovered the principles of radioactivity.)
Poem by Joyce Sidman

CLOSE READ
Notes

1. **READ ▶** As you read lines 1–34, begin to cite text evidence.

• Underline words and phrases in lines 1–6 that reveal the setting.
• In the margin, explain what happens in the last three stanzas.
• Underline details that describe the effect that working with radioactive materials has on Curie.

  First of all, I am a Pole.
Manya, they called me
when I was a girl in Warsaw,
under the dark **yoke** of Russian rule.
5 We hid our Polish grammars
and spit at the obelisk erected by the Tsar.

But I was drawn to Paris
as a plant is drawn to the light.
And the Sorbonne, despite its
10 pointed little men,
shone like the sun itself.
Poverty, prejudice, the infuriating
French language—all this,
like a handful of cobwebs,
15 I swept aside.

yoke:
a wooden frame for harnessing draft animals

Marie Curie goes to study in Paris in spite of numerous obstacles.

97

---

1. **READ AND CITE TEXT EVIDENCE**

A ASK STUDENTS to cite text evidence that describes the setting, plot events, and the main character, Marie Curie. *Students should cite details about the setting from lines 1–6. They should find evidence that Curie overcame obstacles to study in Paris in lines 7–15. They should find evidence that her work to discover radium was difficult (lines 16–24). They should find evidence that the work she valued so much caused serious physical harm (lines 25–34).*

Critical Vocabulary: yoke (line 4) Have students explain how *yoke* is used as a symbol here. How does the narrator, Curie, feel about the Russian rule? *She feels that the Poles were subjugated and were treated poorly.*

CLOSE READ Notes

For the subject of my doctorate,
I chose uranium.
Just a lump of stone—but it shone!
The work was brutal:
20 a ton of ore to be hauled, cracked, **incinerated**
for one pure gram of radium.
I kept a bowl of it at my bedside
so I could wake at night
to its fairy glow.

incinerate:
burn
completely

Marie Curie does "brutal" work as she discovers radium.

25 In the end,
that glow ravaged my skin,
poisoned my blood.
I was like the shell of a burned-out tree.
(B) But what of it?
30 I, Manya,
the poor Polish girl from Warsaw,
pried open life's hidden heart
and discovered the bright burn
of its decay.

Marie Curie's discoveries cause her severe physical harm.

2. ◄ **REREAD AND DISCUSS** Reread lines 1–34. With a small group, discuss details from the poem that convey Curie's pride in her achievements.

SHORT RESPONSE

Cite Text Evidence What do you learn about Marie Curie from the way she responds to her circumstances? Review your reading notes and **cite text evidence** in your response.

Marie Curie is a determined, fearless woman. As a child in Warsaw she faces frightening circumstances "under the dark yoke of Russian rule." She leaves for Paris, where she deals with "Poverty, prejudice, the infuriating French language" and does "brutal" work on the way to making groundbreaking discoveries. Even when her body suffers as a result, she feels it is worthwhile because she achieved so much.

98

TO CHALLENGE STUDENTS . . .

For more context and a deeper understanding of the content of "The Light—Ah! The Light!," students can research the life and work of Marie Curie.

ASK STUDENTS to work with a partner to write an interview with Marie Curie. In each pair, one student will play the part of Curie, and the other will play the part of the interviewer. Each pair of students should identify a unique area of research, so that the class will benefit from a broad understanding of Curie's life and work. For example, assign each pair a period of her life, such as "childhood in Poland," "at the Sorbonne," and "discovery of new elements." Students should conduct their research with the goal of writing three to five interview questions and answers that reveal the most important details about Curie they discover.

After students have completed their research, have them conduct their interviews in front of the class. At the end of the interview, invite the class to ask questions of "Marie Curie" and the interviewer, within the framework of the partners' research. Students will answer the questions if they can, and will take one or two useful questions that they were not able to answer as inspiration for further research.

2. REREAD AND CITE TEXT EVIDENCE

(B) **ASK STUDENTS** to cite text evidence that shows Curie's pride in her achievements. *Students should cite evidence from lines 29–34.*

Critical Vocabulary: incinerate (line 20) Have students determine the meaning of *incinerate* as it is used in the text.

FOR ELL STUDENTS Explain that *ore* is a rock that contains metal. Have a volunteer explain the lines "a ton of ore to be hauled, cracked, incinerated / for one pure gram of radium."

SHORT RESPONSE

Cite Text Evidence Students should:

- show how Curie responds to her circumstances.
- cite textual evidence.
- draw conclusions about Curie based on the evidence.

DIG DEEPER

With the class, return to Question 2, Reread and Discuss. Have students share the results of their discussion.

ASK STUDENTS whether they were satisfied with the outcome of their small-group discussions. Have each group share the evidence they found in the poem that showed Curie's pride in her work, then expand the conversation to include her pride in herself.

- Have volunteers read stanzas of the poem aloud.
- Have volunteers suggest evidence of Curie's pride in her heritage from the first stanza. *Students should cite line 1 as evidence that Curie is proud of being Polish. Share with students that Curie gave the name* polonium *to one of the radioactive elements she discovered, to honor her Polish heritage.*
- Ask students what Curie seems to be proud of in the second stanza. *Students might say she is proud of her courage or strength. Ask them to cite evidence to support their character analysis. Students should cite evidence such as line 15.*
- Ask students what Curie seems to be proud of in the third stanza. *Students might say she is proud of her strength or her curiosity. They should cite evidence such as line 19, "The work was brutal."*
- Ask a volunteer to reread aloud lines 30–35. Ask students if Curie sounds proud in these lines. *Students might say she is proud of her heritage, "Polish girl from Warsaw," of her strength, "pried open," and of her discovery, "discovered the bright burn."*

ASK STUDENTS to return to their Short Response on page 98, and revise their response based on the class discussion.

CLOSE READING NOTES

What Tales Tell

COLLECTION 6
What Tales Tell

"The destiny of the world is determined less by the battles that are lost and won than by the stories it loves and believes in."

—Harold Goddard

Medusa's Head

Greek Myth, retold by Olivia E. Coolidge

Medusa

Poem by Agha Shahid Ali

Why These Texts

Students may read a myth without being aware that it shares many similarities with a short story, such as its use of the fictional elements of setting, characters and a plot with a conflict and a resolution. Students may also not be aware that myths take shape around common themes and that these themes are similar in myths from many different cultures. With the help of the close-reading questions, students will analyze how the same character (Medusa) is treated in two different literary genres—a myth and a poem, noting similarities and differences.

Background Have students read the background and information about Olivia E. Coolidge and Agha Shahid Ali. Introduce the two texts by telling students that Coolidge is best known for her retelling of classical Greek myths for young people, having published her first book, *Greek Myths*, in 1949, at the age of 41, although she began writing as a child. Even though she is famous for her retelling of Greek myths, Coolidge is also known for her biographies of Lincoln, Gandhi, and other political figures.

SETTING A PURPOSE Ask students to pay close attention to the story of Medusa in both the Greek myth and the poem. How soon into the myth can students begin to make an inference about the theme?

 COMMON CORE

Common Core Support

- cite multiple pieces of textual evidence
- determine a theme and how it is conveyed through particular details
- describe how the plot of a myth unfolds in a series of episodes and how the characters respond or change as the plot moves toward a resolution
- summarize key elements of the plot to determine the theme

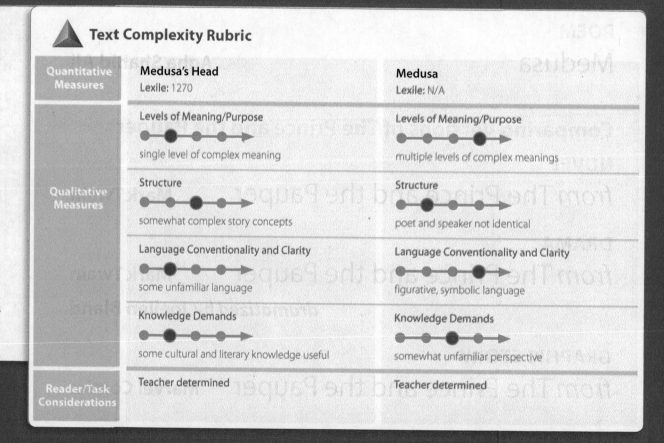

▲ Text Complexity Rubric

		Medusa's Head	Medusa
Quantitative Measures		Lexile: 1270	Lexile: N/A
Qualitative Measures		Levels of Meaning/Purpose	Levels of Meaning/Purpose
		single level of complex meaning	multiple levels of complex meanings
		Structure	Structure
		somewhat complex story concepts	poet and speaker not identical
		Language Conventionality and Clarity	Language Conventionality and Clarity
		some unfamiliar language	figurative, symbolic language
		Knowledge Demands	Knowledge Demands
		some cultural and literary knowledge useful	somewhat unfamiliar perspective
Reader/Task Considerations		Teacher determined	Teacher determined

Determine Theme

Students should read the ancient Greek myth and the contemporary poem carefully all the way through. Close-reading questions at the bottom of the page will help them analyze the two works about Medusa. As they read the two selections, students should record comments or questions about the texts in the side margins.

WHEN STUDENTS STRUGGLE . . .

To help students understand the theme of a myth—an important message (or lesson) about life or human nature—have small groups summarize the main events in a chart such as the one shown as they analyze the myth.

CITE TEXT EVIDENCE For practice in tracing the rising action of a myth to its climax, have students summarize key events to help them determine the theme.

Medusa's Head

- Apollo's prophecy says King Acrisios will have a grandson who will kill him.
- Acrisios locks up his daughter Danae, but Zeus magically enters her room.
- Danae has a son, Perseus, and Acrisios casts the two of them into the sea in a sea chest.
- The gods help, and the chest is found by Dictys, who takes it to King Polydectes.
- Perseus grows up to be strong and handsome.
- King Polydectes fools Perseus into thinking he is getting married, knowing Perseus cannot buy a gift.
- Perseus offers to do anything Polydectes asks, and he is asked to slay the Gorgon Medusa and return with her head.
- Perseus calls on Athene, who will give him Hermes' sword and a shiny shield, warning him to turn his eyes away from the Gorgons so that their gaze will not turn him to stone, and to look at them only in the shield.
- Athene sends him to the sisters Phorcides, whose eye he steals, forcing them to tell him the way to the nymphs.
- Nymphs give him the hat of darkness, winged sandals, and a sack for Medusa's head.
- Perseus reaches the Gorgons' cave, lifts the sword, keeps his eyes on the shield, and kills Medusa, cutting off her head.

Theme: Bravery will be rewarded but cowardice punished.

Background According to Greek myth, Medusa was one of three beautiful sisters known as the Gorgons. The sisters were turned into monsters by Athene, the goddess of wisdom, who was angry at the destruction of one of her temples. Medusa was turned into a horrific creature with a gaping mouth, hypnotic eyes, and hair made of writhing snakes. Anyone who looked into Medusa's eyes was immediately turned to stone.

Medusa's Head

Retold by Olivia E. Coolidge

Medusa

By Agha Shahid Ali

Olivia E. Coolidge (1909–2006) was enjoying a perfectly normal childhood in London with a perfectly normal dislike for Greek literature when she twisted her ankle. For three months a cruel sprain kept her from going outside to play, so she read—and read. Soon she was reading Greek poetry and she made a shocking discovery: she loved it! Coolidge went on to write numerous books of Greek myths for young adults.

Agha Shahid Ali (1949–2001) was born in New Delhi, India, but he lived, studied, and taught in the United States for more than twenty-five years. Ali was a Kashmiri Muslim, but he identified himself as an American poet. Ali's poetry embraces multiple heritages (Hindu, Muslim, and Western) and crosses literary traditions. A joyful, brilliant poet, a man blessed with friends and honors, Ali died from a brain tumor at the age of 52.

101

1. **READ ▶** As you read lines 1–37, begin to collect and cite text evidence.

- Circle what the oracle tells Acrisios.
- Summarize in the margin what Acrisios does to Danae.
- Underline the ways the gods help Danae.
- In the margin, explain Danae's behavior in lines 28–37.

Medusa's Head
Greek Myth retold by Olivia E. Coolidge

King Acrisios of Argos was a hard, selfish man. He hated his brother, Proitos, who later drove him from his kingdom and he cared nothing for his daughter, Danae. His whole heart was set on having a son who should succeed him, but since many years went by and still he had only the one daughter, he sent a message to the oracle of Apollo to ask whether he should have more children of his own. The answer of the oracle was terrible. Acrisios should have no son, but his daughter, Danae, would bear him a grandchild who should grow up to kill him. At these words Acrisios was beside himself with fear

A 10 and rage. Swearing that Danae should never have a child to murder him, he had a room built underground and lined all through with brass. Thither he conducted Danae and shut her up, bidding her spend the rest of her life alone.

Acrisios locks Danae in a sealed room.

It is possible to thwart the plans of mortal men, but never those of

B the gods. Zeus himself looked with pity at the unfortunate girl, and it is said he **descended** to her through the tiny hole that gave light and air to her chamber, pouring himself down into her lap in the form of a shower of gold.

descend:
come down

When word came to the king from those who brought food and

20 drink to his daughter that the girl was with child, Acrisios was angry and afraid. He would have liked best to murder both Danae and her infant son, but he did not dare for fear of the gods' anger at so hideous a crime. He made, therefore, a great chest of wood with bands of brass about it. Shutting up the girl and her baby inside, he cast them into the sea, thinking that they would either drown or starve.

Acrisios shuts Danae and her son in a wooden chest and throws it into the sea.

Again the gods came to the help of Danae, for they caused the planks of the chest to swell until they fitted tightly and let no water in.

The chest floated for some days and was cast up at last on an island. There Dictys, a fisherman, found it and took Danae to his

30 brother, Polydectes, who was king of the island. Danae was made a servant in the palace, yet before many years had passed, both Dictys and Polydectes had fallen in love with the silent, golden-haired girl. She in her heart preferred Dictys, yet since his brother was king, she did not dare to make her choice. Therefore she hung always over Perseus, pretending that mother love left her no room for any other, and year after year a silent frown would cross Polydectes' face as he saw her caress the child.

C At last, Perseus became a young man, handsome and strong beyond the common and a leader among the youths of the island,

40 though he was but the son of a poor servant. Then it seemed to Polydectes that if he could once get rid of Perseus, he could force Danae to become his wife, whether she would or not. Meanwhile, in order to lull the young man's suspicions, he pretended that he intended to marry a certain noble maiden and would collect a wedding gift for her. Now the custom was that this gift of the

Danae gives all her attention to Perseus to avoid having to marry Polydectes.

2. **◀ REREAD** Reread lines 14–27. In what ways are the gods similar to humans? What superhuman powers do they have? Cite textual evidence in your response.

The gods in the story feel human emotions. For instance Zeus "looked with pity" on Danae after she is locked in her room. However, they are able to intervene in human affairs in superhuman ways, such as when Zeus takes the form of a "shower of gold."

3. **READ ▶** As you read lines 38–81, continue to cite textual evidence.

- In lines 38–52, circle Perseus's qualities that suggest he may be a hero.
- In the margin, explain why Polydectes feels "satisfaction" (line 66).
- Underline the items Perseus will use on his journey. In the margin, summarize the steps Perseus must take to slay the Gorgon.

1. **READ AND CITE TEXT EVIDENCE** Explain to students that one way they can determine the theme of a myth is to summarize key events in the plot.

A **ASK STUDENTS** to read their margin notes to a partner and then write one response that best summarizes the action Acrisios takes against Danae, a key event in the development of the plot. *Students should cite specific textual evidence in lines 10–13 and 21–25 to summarize what Acrisios does to Danae to prevent the prophecy from coming true. First, he shuts her up in an underground room. Then, when she does have a son, he encloses them both in a locked wooden chest, which he throws into the sea, thinking they will starve or drown.*

Critical Vocabulary: descend (line 16) Have students share their definitions of *descend* and use it in a sentence.

2. **REREAD AND CITE TEXT EVIDENCE**

B **ASK STUDENTS** for examples of how the Greek gods show their human qualities as well as their supernatural strength and ability to transform themselves, which humans cannot do. *Students should cite evidence in lines 15–18 to highlight not only Zeus's human emotions (he feels "pity" for Danae) but also his superhuman powers (he can turn into a "shower of gold"). Gods can also intervene in human affairs in superhuman ways, as in saving Danae and her son (lines 26–27).*

3. **READ AND CITE TEXT EVIDENCE**

C **ASK STUDENTS** to show how Perseus has the qualities of a mythic hero in that he is handsome, brave, and strong, although of humble birth. *Students should cite details in lines 38–40 to show his heroic qualities, though he is the son of a servant.*

bridegroom to the bride was in part his own and in part put together from the marriage presents of his friends and relatives. All the young men, therefore, brought Polydectes a present, excepting Perseus, who was his servant's son and possessed nothing to bring. Then Polydectes

50 said to the others, "This young man owes me more than any of you, since I took him in and brought him up in my own house, and yet he gives me nothing."

Perseus answered in anger at the injustice of the charge, "I have nothing of my own, Polydectes, yet ask me what you will, and I will fetch it, for I owe you my life."

At this Polydectes smiled, for it was what he had intended, and he answered, "Fetch me, if this is your boast, the Gorgon's head."

Now the Gorgons, who lived far off on the shores of the ocean, were three fearful sisters with hands of brass, wings of gold, and

60 scales like a serpent. Two of them had scaly heads and tusks like the wild boar, but the third, Medusa, had the face of a beautiful woman with hair of writhing serpents, and so terrible was her expression that all who looked on it were immediately turned to stone. This much Perseus knew of the Gorgons, but of how to find or kill them, he had

(D) no idea. Nevertheless he had given his promise, and though he saw now the satisfaction of King Polydectes, he was bound to keep his word. In his perplexity he prayed to the wise goddess, Athene, who came to him in a vision and promised him her aid.

"First, you must go," she said, "to the sisters Phorcides, who will

70 tell you the way to the nymphs who guard the hat of darkness, the winged sandals, and the knapsack which can hold the Gorgon's head. Then I will give you a shield and my brother, Hermes, a sword which shall be made of adamant, the hardest rock. For nothing else can kill the Gorgon, since so venomous is her blood that a mortal sword when plunged in it is eaten away. But when you come to the Gorgons, invisible in your hat of darkness, turn your eyes away from them and look only on their reflection in your gleaming shield. Thus you may kill the monster without yourself being turned to stone. Pass her sisters by, for they are immortal, but smite off the head of Medusa

80 with the hair of writhing snakes. Then put it in your knapsack and return, and I will be with you."

Polydectes is satisfied because Perseus has left the island on a very dangerous mission.

1. Go to the sisters Phorcides.
2. Get the hat of darkness, winged sandals, and knapsack.
3. Take the shield from Athena and the sword from Hermes.
4. Kill the Gorgon while his face is turned away.

The vision ended, and with the aid of Athene, Perseus set out on the long journey to seek the Phorcides. These live in a dim cavern in the far north, where nights and days are one and where the whole earth is overspread with perpetual twilight. There sat the three old women mumbling to one another, crouched in a dim heap together, for they had but one eye and one tooth between them which they passed from hand to hand. Perseus came quietly behind them, and as they fumbled for the eye, he put his strong, brown hand next to one of

90 the long, yellow ones, so that the old crone thought that it was her sister's and put the eye in it. There was a high scream of anger when they discovered the theft, and much clawing and groping in the dim recesses of the cavern. But they were helpless in their blindness and Perseus could laugh at them. At length for the price of their eye they told him how to reach the nymphs, and Perseus, laying the eye quickly in the hand of the nearest sister, fled as fast as he could before she could use it.

Again it was a far journey to the garden of the nymphs, where it is always sunshine and the trees bear golden apples. But the nymphs are

100 friends of the wise gods and hate the monsters of darkness and the spirits of anger and despair. Therefore, they received Perseus with rejoicing and put the hat of darkness on his head, while on his feet they bound the golden, winged sandals, which are those Hermes wears when he runs down the slanting sunbeams or races along the

The Phorcides help Perseus because they need their eye back.

The nymphs are friends with the gods, who are helping Perseus. They hate monsters, including the Gorgons.

4. **◀ REREAD** Reread lines 53–68. What is heroic about the way Perseus responds to the request Polydectes makes? Support your answer with explicit textual evidence.

Even when Perseus realizes that Polydectes wants to send him away unjustly, he honors his word. He recognizes the challenge ahead and prays to Athene for help.

5. **READ ▶** As you read lines 82–154, continue to cite textual evidence.

• In the margin, explain why the Phorcides and the nymphs help Perseus.

• Underline details that create concern for Perseus.

• Circle the text that may be the climax—the exciting point in a story where a conflict is about to be resolved.

WHEN STUDENTS STRUGGLE . . .

To help students understand how the theme of a story or myth is a message (or lesson) about life or human nature, ask them to reread lines 38–81. Invite them to work with a small group to discuss how this section that introduces Perseus's quest gives insight into the theme of the myth.

FOR ELL STUDENTS Explain that a phrasal verb is followed by a preposition, which gives the verb another meaning, and that phrasal verbs may be difficult for ELL students to understand. Point out that several phrasal verbs are created from the verb *turn*. Tell students (or elicit) the meaning of *turn to (stone)* (line 63) and *turn (your eyes) away* (line 76). *Turn to* means "to change into" and *turn away* means "to move in a different direction so as not to see something." Ask students to use each phrasal verb in a sentence.

4. **REREAD AND CITE TEXT EVIDENCE** Explain that a mythic hero often goes on a quest (or journey) to accomplish a dangerous task.

(D) **ASK STUDENTS** to cite specific textual evidence to demonstrate the heroic way in which Perseus keeps his word to Polydectes. *Students should cite explicit evidence from lines 65–68 to show that despite the fact that Perseus realizes that the king is sending him away unjustly, he keeps his word to bring back the Gorgon's head. To help with the quest, he calls on Athene to help.*

5. **READ AND CITE TEXT EVIDENCE**

(E) **ASK STUDENTS** to tell at which point in the story the action rises to its highest point, and readers feel the most emotion. *Students should cite textual evidence from lines 139–141 to point out that this is the climax of the story, the point at which the conflict with the Gorgons is about to be resolved.*

CLOSE READ
Notes

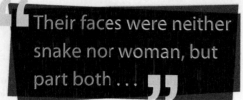

"Their faces were neither snake nor woman, but part both . . ."

pathways of the wind. Next, Perseus put on his back the silver sack with the gleaming tassels of gold and flung across his shoulder the black-sheathed sword that was the gift of Hermes. On his left arm he fitted the shield that Athene gave, a gleaming silver shield like a mirror, plain without any marking. Then he sprang into the air and
110 ran, invisible like the rushing wind, far out over the white-capped sea, across the yellow sands of the eastern desert, over strange streams and towering mountains, until at last he came to the shores of the distant ocean which flowed round all the world.

There was a grey gorge of stone by the ocean's edge, where lay Medusa and her sisters sleeping in the dim depths of the rock. All up and down the cleft the stones took fantastic shapes of trees, beasts, birds, or serpents. Here and there a man who had looked on the terrible Medusa stood forever with horror on his face. Far over the twilit gorge Perseus **hovered** invisible, while he loosened the pale,
120 strange sword from its black sheath. Then with his face turned away and eyes on the silver shield he dropped, slow and silent as a falling leaf, down through the rocky cleft, twisting and turning past countless strange grey shapes, down from the bright sunlight into a chill, dim shadow echoing and re-echoing with the dashing of waves on the tumbled rocks beneath. There on the heaped stones lay the Gorgons sleeping together in the dimness, and even as he looked on them in the shield, Perseus felt stiff with horror at the sight.

F   Two of the Gorgons lay sprawled together, shaped like women yet scaled from head to foot as serpents are. Instead of hands they had
130 gleaming claws like eagles, and their feet were dragons' feet. Skinny metallic wings like bats' wings hung from their shoulders. Their faces were neither snake nor woman, but part both, like faces in a nightmare. These two lay arm in arm and never stirred. Only the blue snakes still hissed and writhed round the pale, set face of Medusa, as

hover:

stay suspended in the air

106

---

though even in sleep she were troubled by an evil dream. She lay by herself, arms outstretched, face upwards, more beautiful and terrible than living man may bear. All the crimes and madnesses of the world rushed into Perseus' mind as he gazed at her image in the shield.
E   Horror stiffened his arm as he hovered over her with his sword
140 uplifted. Then he shut his eyes to the vision and in the darkness struck.

There was a great cry and a hissing. Perseus groped for the head and seized it by the limp and snaky hair. Somehow he put it in his knapsack and was up and off, for at the dreadful scream the sister Gorgons had awakened. Now they were after him, their sharp claws grating against his silver shield. Perseus strained forward on the pathway of the wind like a runner, and behind him the two sisters came, smelling out the prey they could not see. Snakes darted from their girdles,[1] foam flew from their tusks, and the great wings beat the
150 air. Yet the winged sandals were even swifter than they, and Perseus fled like the hunted deer with the speed of desperation. Presently the horrible noise grew faint behind him, the hissing of snakes and the sound of the bat wings died away. At last the Gorgons could smell him no longer and returned home unavenged.

[1] **girdles:** belts.

6. ◀ REREAD   Reread lines 128–154. The resolution of a conflict may suggest a work's theme. What theme might be suggested by Perseus's triumph?

The resolution suggests that if you keep your word, act bravely, and obey the gods, you can triumph and achieve great things.

CLOSE READ
Notes

107

Critical Vocabulary: hover (line 119) Have students share their definitions of *hover*. What does the narrator mean by saying, "Far over the twilit gorge Perseus hovered invisible, while he loosened the pale, strange sword from its black sheath"? *The narrator means that while invisible, Perseus stays suspended in midair while he removes the unusual sword from its covering. Ask students to give examples of other things that hover, such as helicopters, and to create a sentence for each.*

6.   REREAD AND CITE TEXT EVIDENCE   Point out that the resolution of a conflict takes place after the climax and is part of the falling action of the plot.

F   ASK STUDENTS to reread lines 128–154, paying close attention to lines 139–141, the climax of the story, and have them paraphrase how the conflict with the Gorgons is resolved. Then lead them to recognize that the resolution of the conflict begins with line 142, which signals the falling action in the second half of the story. Remind students that Perseus has performed a great feat. Ask students to consider the theme that might be represented by his triumphant success. *Students should be able to recognize that the resolution of the conflict suggests the theme that brave deeds will be rewarded.*

G By now Perseus was over the Lybian desert, and as the blood from the horrible head touched the sand, it changed to serpents, from which the snakes of Africa are descended.

H The storms of the Lybian desert blew against Perseus in clouds of eddying sand, until not even the divine sandals could hold him on his
160 course. Far out to sea he was blown, and then north. Finally, whirled around the heavens like a cloud of mist, he alighted in the distant west where the giant, Atlas, held up on his shoulders the heavens from the earth. There the weary giant, crushed under the load of centuries, begged Perseus to show him Medusa's head. Perseus uncovered for him the dreadful thing, and Atlas was changed to the mighty mountain whose rocks rear up to reach the sky near the gateway to the Atlantic. Perseus himself, returning eastwards and still battling with the wind, was driven south to the land of Ethiopia, where king Cepheus reigned with his wife, Cassiopeia.

170 As Perseus came wheeling in like a gull from the ocean, he saw a strange sight. Far out to sea the water was troubled, seething and boiling as though stirred by a great force moving in its depths. Huge, sullen waves were starting far out and washing inland over sunken trees and flooded houses. Many miles of land were under water, and as he sped over them, he saw the muddy sea lapping around the foot of a black, upstanding rock. Here on a ledge above the water's edge stood a young girl chained by the arms, lips parted, eyes open and staring, face white as her linen garment. She might have been a statue, so still she stood, while the light breeze fluttered her dress and stirred
180 her loosened hair. As Perseus looked at her and looked at the sea, the water began to boil again, and miles out a long, grey scaly back of vast length lifted itself above the flood. At that there was a shriek from a distant knoll where he could dimly see the forms of people, but the

---

girl shrank a little and said nothing. Then Perseus, taking off the hat of darkness, alighted near the maiden to talk to her, and she, though nearly mad with terror, found words at last to tell him her tale.

I Her name was Andromeda, and she was the only child of the king and of his wife, Cassiopeia. Queen Cassiopeia was exceedingly beautiful, so that all people marveled at her. She herself was proud of
190 her dark eyes, her white, slender fingers, and her long black hair, so proud that she had been heard to boast that she was fairer even than the sea nymphs who are daughters of Nereus. At this Nereus in **wrath** stirred up Poseidon,[2] who came flooding in over the land, covering it far and wide. Not content with this he sent a vast monster from the dark depths of the bottomless sea to ravage the whole coast of Ethiopia. When the unfortunate king and queen had sought the advice of the oracle on how to appease the god, they had been ordered to sacrifice their only daughter to the sea monster Poseidon had sent. Not daring for their people's sake to disobey, they had chained her to
200 this rock, where she now awaited the beast who should devour her.

J Perseus comforted Andromeda as he stood by her on the rock, and she shrank closer against him while the great, grey back writhed its half-mile length slowly towards the land. Then bidding Andromeda hide her face, Perseus sprang once more into the air,

---

[2] **Poseidon:** in Greek mythology, the god of the seas.

---

wrath:
anger; fury

Andromeda's parents tied her to a rock as a sacrifice to the gods.

---

8. ◀ **REREAD** Reread lines 158–169. Why does Atlas beg Perseus to show him Medusa's head? Cite explicit textual evidence in your response.

Atlas is "crushed under the load of centuries" from holding up the heavens. He wants to look at Medusa's head because he will not feel pain if he is turned to stone.

---

7. **READ** ▶ As you read lines 155–186, continue to cite text evidence.
- Circle the explanation of the origin of something found in nature.
- Underline what happens when Perseus shows Medusa's head to Atlas.
- Circle the author's description of the young girl in lines 170–186.

9. **READ** ▶ As you read lines 187–212, continue to cite text evidence.
- Circle what Queen Cassiopeia does to make Nereus so angry.
- In the margin, summarize what has happened to Andromeda in lines 187–200.
- Underline what happens when Perseus shows Medusa's head to the sea monster.

---

7. **READ AND CITE TEXT EVIDENCE** Point out that myths explain how and why things in nature came to be.

G **ASK STUDENTS** to play close attention to lines 155–157 and 165–167 to explain how the ancient Greeks used this myth to account for how these things came to be in nature: the snakes in Africa and the mighty "mountain . . . near the gateway to the Atlantic." *Students should cite specific textual evidence in lines 155–157 and 165–167 to recognize that according to this Greek myth, while Perseus was flying over the Lybian desert, the blood from Medusa's head touched the sand and was changed into serpents, which is how the snakes of Africa came to be; when Perseus uncovered Medusa's head for the giant Atlas, who was holding up the heavens, Atlas was changed into the mighty Atlas Mountains, which still bear his name.*

8. **REREAD AND CITE TEXT EVIDENCE**

H **ASK STUDENTS** to draw an inference from lines 158–167 to suggest why the weary giant Atlas, who was holding up the heavens, may have pleaded with Perseus to show him the head of Medusa. *Students should infer that Atlas may have wanted to look at Medusa's head so that he can be turned to stone in order not to feel the heavy weight.*

9. **READ AND CITE TEXT EVIDENCE** .

I **ASK STUDENTS** to read their margin notes to a partner and write one response to summarize the events leading to Andromeda's being chained to a rock above the water's edge. *Students should cite specific textual evidence from lines 187–200 to summarize the events, beginning with Cassiopeia's insult to Nereus's daughters.*

Critical Vocabulary: wrath (line 192) Have students define *wrath* and use it in a sentence.

unveiling the dreadful head of dead Medusa to the monster which reared its dripping jaws yards high into the air. The mighty tail stiffened all of a sudden, the boiling of the water ceased, and only the gentle waves of the receding ocean lapped around a long, grey ridge of stone. Then Perseus freed Andromeda and restored her to her father

210 and beautiful mother. Thereafter with their consent he married her amid scenes of tremendous rejoicing, and with his bride set sail at last for the kingdom of Polydectes.

Polydectes had lost no time on the departure of Perseus. First he had begged Danae to become his wife, and then he had threatened her. Undoubtedly he would have got his way by force if Danae had not fled in terror to Dictys. The two took refuge at the altar of a temple whence Polydectes did not dare drag them away. So matters stood when Perseus returned. Polydectes was enraged to see him, for he had hoped at least that Danae's most powerful protector would never

220 return. But now, seeing him famous and with a king's daughter to wife, he could not contain himself. Openly he laughed at the tale of Perseus, saying that the hero had never killed the Gorgon, only pretended to, and that now he was claiming an honor he did not

10. ◀ **REREAD** Reread lines 201–212. What is heroic about Perseus's rescue of Andromeda?

He saves Andromeda from her unjust punishment and preserves her parents' kingdom. He uses supernatural powers and Medusa's head to defeat a fearsome creature.

11. **READ** ▶ As you read lines 213–252, continue to cite textual evidence.

• Circle the resolution of the conflict between Perseus and Polydectes.
• Underline Perseus's action in lines 228–235 that shows his gratitude to the gods.
• In the margin, explain how the earlier prophecy of Apollo is fulfilled in lines 242–252.

110

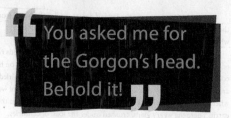

> "You asked me for the Gorgon's head. Behold it!"

deserve. At this Perseus, enraged by the insult and by reports of his mother's persecution, said to him, "You asked me for the Gorgon's head. Behold it!" And with that he lifted it high, and Polydectes became stone.

Then Perseus left Dictys to be king of that island, but he himself went back to the Grecian mainland to seek out his grandfather,

230 Acrisios, who was once again king of Argos. First, however, he gave back to the gods the gifts they had given him. Hermes took back the golden sandals and the hat of darkness, for both are his. But Athene took Medusa's head, and she hung it on a fleece around her neck as part of her battle equipment, where it may be seen in statues and portraits of the warlike goddess.

Perseus took ship for Greece, but his fame had gone before him, and king Acrisios fled secretly from Argos in terror, since he remembered the prophecy and feared that Perseus had come to avenge the wrongs of Danae. The trembling old Acrisios took refuge

240 in Larissa, where it happened the king was holding a great athletic contest in honor of his dead father.

Heroes from all over Greece, among whom was Perseus, came to the games. As Perseus was competing at the discus throwing, he threw high into the air and far beyond the rest. A strong wind caught the discus as it spun so that it left the course marked out for it and was carried into the stands. People scrambled away to right and left.

111

10. REREAD AND CITE TEXT EVIDENCE

J ASK STUDENTS to cite specific textual evidence to illustrate how Perseus uses his intelligence, courage, strength, and supernatural powers to rescue Andromeda from Poseidon's sea monster. *Students should cite evidence from lines 203–209 to highlight how Perseus acts heroically to free Andromeda from her unjust fate by cleverly uncovering Medusa's head to turn the sea creature to stone; students should also cite evidence from lines 210–212 to show how he restores Andromeda to her parents, preserves her parents' kingdom, and marries the princess—all aspects of the mythic hero.*

11. READ AND CITE TEXT EVIDENCE

K ASK STUDENTS to work with a partner to write one response to state how Apollo's oracle is fulfilled, as Acrisios is killed by his grandson Perseus. *Students should cite specific textual evidence from lines 242–252 to show that Acrisios is killed by the discus Perseus throws at the athletic games, fulfilling the prophecy.*

WHEN STUDENTS STRUGGLE . . .

To help students understand how the theme—the message (or lesson) about life or human nature—can be determined in a myth, have students ask themselves these questions: *What is the lesson the myth teaches? How is this message conveyed by the characters' flaws, mistakes, or triumphs or by the action of the plot?* Invite students to work with a small group to discuss how students can infer the theme of this myth from Perseus's positive character traits and actions.

FOR ELL STUDENTS In order for students to understand this section in the falling action of the story, suggest that they use context clues to try to determine the meaning of these words and phrases: *Behold it!* (line 226), *battle equipment* (line 234), *athletic contest* (lines 240–241), *discus throwing* (line 243), *nimble* (line 247), *feeble* (line 248), and *prophecy* (line 249).

Though Perseus did not intend it, his discus kills Acrisios.

Only Acrisios was not nimble enough. The heavy weight fell full on his foot and crushed his toes, and at that the feeble old man, already weakened by his terrors, died from the shock. Thus the prophecy of
250 Apollo was fulfilled at last; Acrisios was killed by his grandson. Then Perseus came into his kingdom, where he reigned with Andromeda long and happily.

12. ◀ REREAD AND DISCUSS Reread lines 228–252. In a small group, discuss what is ironic, or unexpected, about Acrisios's death. Cite explicit textual evidence in your discussion.

SHORT RESPONSE

Cite Text Evidence What theme, or central idea about life, is expressed in this myth? Consider the way conflicts are resolved and the way characters behave. Review your reading notes and **cite text evidence** in your response.

The myth expresses the theme that bravery will be rewarded and cowardice will be punished. Perseus is sent on a dangerous mission to fetch the Gorgon's head. He did not know how to complete the mission but with the help of the gods he is able to escape harm and win the conflict. Perseus is also brave when he defeats a dangerous sea monster. He is rewarded when he takes Andromeda as his bride. On the other hand, characters such as Polydectes and Acrisios behave in a cowardly way and are punished. Polydectes mistreats and threatens Danae before going into hiding. He is punished when Perseus turns him to stone. Likewise, Acrisios flees from Argos to escape the fate the gods prophesized, but he is killed.

112

---

1. READ ▶ As you read lines 1–36 of the poem, collect and cite text evidence.

- Circle the questions Medusa asks.
- In lines 15–27, underline what Medusa threatens to do. In the margin, make an inference about her character.
- In the margin, summarize what happens in the last stanza.

Medusa
Poem by Agha Shahid Ali

B "I must be beautiful.
Or why would men be speechless
at my sight? I have populated the countryside
with animals of stone
5 and put nations painlessly to sleep.
I too was human, I who now live here
at the end of the world
with two aging sisters, spinsters
massaging poisons into our scalps
10 and sunning our ruffled snakes,

and dreading the night, when
under the warm stars
we recall men we have loved,
their gestures now forever refusing us.

A 15 Then why let anything remain
when whatever we loved
turned instantly to stone?
I am waiting for the Mediterranean
to see me: It will petrify.
20 And as caravans from Africa begin to cross it,
I will freeze their cargo of slaves.

Medusa is angry that she has been turned into a monster who cannot find love. In her anger, she wants revenge on the world.

113

---

12. REREAD AND DISCUSS USING TEXT EVIDENCE

L **ASK STUDENTS** to appoint a reporter for each group to cite specific textual evidence and line numbers to evaluate the effectiveness of the use of irony (or an unexpected situation) in the death of Acrisios. How does it fulfill the prophecy in an unexpected (and humorous) way? *Students should cite specific textual evidence from lines 242–252 to demonstrate the ironic situation implicit in the fact that Acrisios dies as a result of Perseus's throwing the discus, which lands on the feeble man's feet.*

SHORT RESPONSE

Cite Text Evidence Students should cite evidence from the text to support their view of the theme. Students should:

- explain the theme, or central idea about life.
- give reasons for their point of view.
- cite specific textual evidence to support their reasons.

1. READ AND CITE TEXT EVIDENCE

A **ASK STUDENTS** to read their margin notes to a partner and write one response that makes an inference about Medusa's character based on the threats she makes in lines 15–27. Point out that students should use what they already know about Medusa from the myth and combine it with specific evidence from the poem in order to make an inference about her character. *Students should cite explicit textual evidence from lines 15–27 to highlight how Medusa will use her power to turn anyone or anything that looks upon her to stone, so that she may seek her revenge upon the world for having turned her and her sisters into monsters whom no one can love.*

FOR ELL STUDENTS Point out that the word *to* (line 5) is a homophone, a word that sounds like another word but has a different meaning and spelling. Ask students to find and cite both homophones of *to* in the poem (lines 6 and 8).

CLOSE READ
Notes

Soon, soon, the sky will have eyes:
I will fossilize its dome into cracked blue,
I who am about to come
25   into God's full view
from the wrong side of the mirror
into which He gazes."

And so she dreams
till the sun-crimsoned shield
30   blinds her into nightmare;
her locks, failing from their roots,
crawl into rocks to die.
Perseus holds the sword above her neck.
Restless in her sleep, she,
35   for the last time, brushes back
the hissing curls from her forehead.

Perseus is about to slay Medusa, who has fallen asleep for the last time.

2. **◀ REREAD AND DISCUSS** With a small group, discuss the way Medusa is presented in the poem. In what way does learning her thoughts and feelings affect your view of her? Cite text evidence in your discussion.

SHORT RESPONSE

Cite Text Evidence How do "Medusa's Head" and "Medusa" differ in their presentation of Medusa? Review your reading notes, and be sure to **cite evidence from the text** in your response.

In "Medusa's Head," Medusa is a monster and Perseus is the hero who destroys her. We only see her briefly and we do not learn her thoughts and feelings. In "Medusa," the poet delves deeply into her character. We learn she is sad and angry about her curse and longs to be able to love again. We are more able to relate to Medusa in the poem because we learn her feelings.

114

---

2. **REREAD AND DISCUSS USING TEXT EVIDENCE**

B ASK STUDENTS to appoint a reporter for each group to cite specific textual evidence and line numbers to discuss and evaluate the effectiveness of the way in which Medusa is presented in the poem. How do her human qualities of expressing her thoughts and feelings heighten the audience's emotions, enabling them to feel pity for her and influencing their point of view? *Students should cite evidence in lines 1–14 to describe her recollections, lines 15–27 to depict her anger and revenge, and lines 28–36 to portray her death at Perseus's hand.*

SHORT RESPONSE

Cite Text Evidence Students should cite explicit evidence from the text to support their positions. Students should:

- explain how the two treatments of Medusa differ.
- give reasons for their point of view.
- cite evidence from the text to support their reasons.

TO CHALLENGE STUDENTS . . .

For more context, and a richer understanding of the gods and goddesses as well as the heroes and monsters of Greek mythology, students can view the video titled "Greek Gods" in their eBooks.

ASK STUDENTS to do some preliminary research to find out more information about Perseus, Medusa, or another Greek god, goddess, hero, or monster mentioned in the myth. Possible topics for their research report might be:

- further exploits of Perseus
- the Gorgons and other monsters in Greek mythology
- Greek gods and heroes

With the class, discuss these elements of a research report after students have chosen a topic.

- Plan Your Research
  —Write questions about your topic.
  —Research your topic and take notes.
  —Organize your notes.
  —Write an outline based on your notes.
- Write Your Report
  —Keep your purpose and audience in mind.
  —Write a first draft, revise your report, and proofread it.
  —Reread your report and check that your bibliography is accurate.
- Publish and Share
  —Make a final copy of your report.
  —Publish and share it.

ASK STUDENTS what they hope to discover as they research their report. How is the information they find similar to yet different from the story and details shared by the myth and the poem about Medusa?

DIG DEEPER

1. With the class, return to Question 12, Reread and Discuss, in "Medusa's Head." Have students share the results of their discussion.

ASK STUDENTS whether they were pleased with the outcome of their small-group discussions. Have each group share how it defined irony and what it identified as being unexpected about the death of Acrisios. What was ironic (and almost humorous) about the situation in which he died? Have each group cite the specific textual evidence it found to support its viewpoint.

- Encourage students to tell whether there was any compelling evidence cited by group members holding a different opinion. If so, why didn't it sway the group?
- How did the group resolve any differences of opinion?
- After students have shared the results of their discussion, ask whether another group shared any ideas they wish they had thought of.

ASK STUDENTS to return to their Short Response answer and to revise it based on the class discussion of the myth.

2. With the class, return to Question 2, Reread and Discuss, in the poem "Medusa." Have students share the results of their discussion.

ASK STUDENTS whether they were pleased with the outcome of their small-group discussions. Have each group share its view concerning how Medusa is presented in the poem, and how knowing her thoughts and feelings influenced their point of view of her. What evidence did each group cite from the poem to support its viewpoint?

- Encourage students to tell whether there was any covincing evidence cited by group members holding a different opinion. If so, why didn't it sway the group's point of view of Medusa in the poem? How did the group use conflict-resolution techniques to solve any disagreements?
- After groups have shared the results of their discussion, ask whether another group shared any findings they wished they had brought to the table.

ASK STUDENTS to return to their Short Response answer and to revise it based on the class discussion about the presentation of Medusa in the poem.

CLOSE READING NOTES

Comparing Versions

The Prince and the Pauper
from the Novel by Mark Twain

The Prince and the Pauper
Dramatization by Joellen Bland

The Prince and the Pauper
Graphic Story by Marvel Comics

Why These Texts

Students can practice close reading by comparing versions of a scene from Mark Twain's novel with dramatic and graphic versions. With the help of the close-reading questions, students will analyze the excerpt in each of the three forms, compare them, and consider the advantages of one form over the other.

Background Have students read the background and the information about the authors. Tell them that they will read three versions of a scene from a novel by Mark Twain: Twain's version; a dramatization by Joellen Bland; and a Marvel Comics graphic version. In a previous chapter, two boys are born on the same day. One is rich, one is poor. One is wanted, one is not.

SETTING A PURPOSE Ask students to pay attention to similarities and differences between the prince and the pauper. How are they presented in each version of the scene?

Common Core Support

- cite textual evidence
- describe how characters change as the plot moves forward
- analyze how a scene contributes to the development of the plot
- compare and contrast different versions of a scene

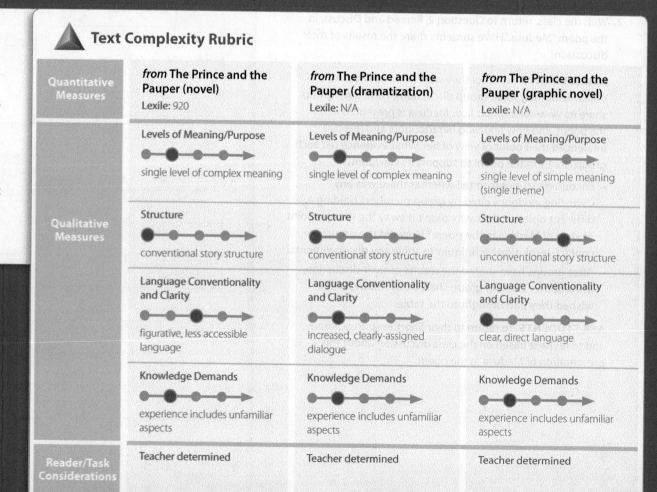

Text Complexity Rubric

	from The Prince and the Pauper (novel) Lexile: 920	*from* The Prince and the Pauper (dramatization) Lexile: N/A	*from* The Prince and the Pauper (graphic novel) Lexile: N/A
Quantitative Measures			
Qualitative Measures	Levels of Meaning/Purpose single level of complex meaning	Levels of Meaning/Purpose single level of complex meaning	Levels of Meaning/Purpose single level of simple meaning (single theme)
	Structure conventional story structure	Structure conventional story structure	Structure unconventional story structure
	Language Conventionality and Clarity figurative, less accessible language	Language Conventionality and Clarity increased, clearly-assigned dialogue	Language Conventionality and Clarity clear, direct language
	Knowledge Demands experience includes unfamiliar aspects	Knowledge Demands experience includes unfamiliar aspects	Knowledge Demands experience includes unfamiliar aspects
Reader/Task Considerations	Teacher determined	Teacher determined	Teacher determined

Compare Versions of a Text

Students should read all three versions of this scene carefully all the way through. Close-reading questions at the bottom of the page will help them focus on a thorough analysis of the texts. As they read, students should jot down comments or questions about the texts in the side margins.

WHEN STUDENTS STRUGGLE . . .

To help students compare three versions of "The Prince and the Pauper," have them work in a small group to fill out charts, such as the ones shown below, as they analyze the texts.

CITE TEXT EVIDENCE For practice comparing and contrasting versions of a story, ask students to cite evidence of similarities and differences in each version of the scene. Also, ask students to describe *how* each version presents information about the characters.

Novel Version	
How do you learn about the characters? *The characters are described in the text.*	
One similarity between the prince and the pauper: They have "the same eyes, the same voice and manner, the same form and stature, the same face and countenance."	*One difference between the prince and the pauper: The pauper dressed "in his rags," whereas the prince's "clothing was all of lovely silks and satins."*

Dramatic Version	
How do you learn about the characters? *through dialogue and stage directions*	
One similarity between the prince and the pauper: They both would like to "play in the mud."	*One difference: Sometimes the pauper is "hungry," but the prince's palace has a "bowl of nuts."*

Graphic Version	
How do you learn about the characters? *from pictures as well as words*	
One similarity between the prince and the pauper: They look like twins.	*One difference: The guard treats the pauper roughly, but he follows the orders of the prince.*

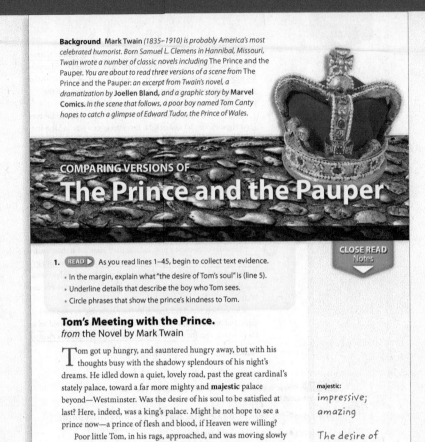

Background Mark Twain *(1835–1910) is probably America's most celebrated humorist. Born Samuel L. Clemens in Hannibal, Missouri, Twain wrote a number of classic novels including The Prince and the Pauper. You are about to read three versions of a scene from* The Prince and the Pauper: *an excerpt from Twain's novel, a dramatization by* **Joellen Bland,** *and a graphic story by* **Marvel Comics.** *In the scene that follows, a poor boy named Tom Canty hopes to catch a glimpse of Edward Tudor, the Prince of Wales.*

COMPARING VERSIONS OF
The Prince and the Pauper

CLOSE READ
Notes

1. **READ ▷** As you read lines 1–45, begin to collect text evidence.
   - In the margin, explain what "the desire of Tom's soul" is (line 5).
   - Underline details that describe the boy who Tom sees.
   - Circle phrases that show the prince's kindness to Tom.

Tom's Meeting with the Prince.
from the Novel by Mark Twain

Tom got up hungry, and sauntered hungry away, but with his thoughts busy with the shadowy splendours of his night's dreams. He idled down a quiet, lovely road, past the great cardinal's stately palace, toward a far more mighty and **majestic** palace beyond—Westminster. Was the desire of his soul to be satisfied at last? Here, indeed, was a king's palace. Might he not hope to see a prince now—a prince of flesh and blood, if Heaven were willing?

Poor little Tom, in his rags, approached, and was moving slowly and timidly past the sentinels, with a beating heart and a rising hope, when all at once he caught sight through the golden bars of a spectacle that almost made him shout for joy. Within was a comely boy, <u>tanned and brown with sturdy outdoor sports and exercises, whose clothing was all of lovely silks and satins, shining with jewels; at his hip a little jewelled sword and dagger; dainty buskins[1] on his feet, with red heels;</u>

majestic:
impressive;
amazing

The desire of Tom's soul is to see a prince in person.

10
(A)

---
[1] **buskin:** thick-soled laced boot that reaches to the calf.

115

1. **READ AND CITE TEXT EVIDENCE**

(A) **ASK STUDENTS** to use their marked text as evidence and describe the prince. *Students should cite underlined text in lines 11–17 as evidence of the prince's wealthy appearance and circled text in lines 28–32, 38, 40–41, and 43–44 as evidence of his kindness.*

Critical Vocabulary: majestic (line 4) Have students determine the meaning of *majestic* as it is used here. Ask students to compare *majestic* and the related word *grand*. What connotations does *majestic* have that *grand* does not? Why might Twain have chosen to use *majestic* to describe the palace? *The word* majestic *has to do with royalty (a king may be called "His Majesty"), and the palace is the home of the royal family.*

CLOSE READ
Notes

and on his head a jaunty crimson cap, with drooping plumes fastened with a great sparkling gem. Several gorgeous gentlemen stood near— his servants, without a doubt, Oh! He was a prince—a prince, a living prince, a real prince—without the shadow of a question; and the prayer of the pauper-boy's heart was answered at last.

20   Tom's breath came quick and short with excitement, and his eyes grew big with wonder and delight. Everything gave way in his mind instantly to one desire: that was to get close to the prince, and have a good, devouring look at him. Before he knew what he was about, he had his face against the gate-bars. The next instant one of the soldiers snatched him rudely away, and sent him spinning among the gaping crowd of country gawks and London idlers. The soldier said,—

      "Mind thy manners, thou young beggar!"

      The crowd jeered and laughed; but the young prince sprang to the gate with his face flushed, and his eyes flashing with indignation, and
30 cried out,—

B   "How dar'st thou use a poor lad like that? How dar'st thou use the King my father's meanest subject so? Open the gates, and let him in!"

      You should have seen that fickle crowd snatch off their hats then. You should have heard them cheer, and shout, "Long live the Prince of Wales!"

      The soldiers presented arms with their halberds,[2] opened the gates, and presented again as the little Prince of Poverty passed in, in his fluttering rags, to join hands with the Prince of Limitless Plenty.

---

[2] **halberd:** a weapon that resembles a battle-ax.

---

2. ◀ **REREAD** Reread lines 27–41. What does the prince's treatment of Tom reveal about his character? Cite text evidence in your response.

The prince invites Tom into the palace after scolding the guard,
which suggests he is fair and humble.

3. **READ** ▶ As you read lines 46–111, continue to cite text evidence.

- Underline the questions the prince asks Tom.
- In the margin, describe the prince's reaction to what Tom says in lines 57–64.
- Circle the prince's reactions to Tom's description of home in lines 79–111. In the margin, paraphrase what the prince says in lines 102–105.

116

Edward Tudor said—

40   "Thou lookest tired and hungry: thou'st been treated ill. Come with me."

      Edward took Tom to a rich apartment in the palace, which he called his cabinet. By his command a repast was brought such as Tom had never encountered before except in books. The prince sat near by, and asked questions while Tom ate.

      "What is thy name, lad?"

      "Tom Canty, an' it please thee, sir."

      "'Tis an odd one. Where dost live?"

      "In the city, please thee, sir. Offal[3] Court, out of Pudding Lane."

50   "Offal Court! Truly 'tis another odd one. Hast parents?"

      "Parents have I, sir, and a grand-dam likewise that is but indifferently precious to me, God forgive me if it be offence to say it—also twin sisters, Nan and Bet."

      "Then is thy grand-dam not over kind to thee, I take it?"

      "Neither to any other is she, so please your worship."

      "Doth she mistreat thee?"

      "There be times that she stayeth her hand, being asleep or overcome with drink; but when she hath her judgment clear again, she maketh it up to me with goodly beatings."

C 60   A fierce look came into the little prince's eyes, and he cried out—

      "What! Beatings?"

      "Oh, indeed, yes, please you, sir."

      "Beatings!—and thou so frail and little. Is thy father kind to thee?"

      "Not more than Gammer Canty, sir."

      "Fathers be alike, mayhap. Mine hath not a doll's temper. He smiteth with a heavy hand, yet spareth me: he spareth me not always with his tongue, though, sooth to say. How doth thy mother use thee?"

      "She is good, sir, and giveth me neither sorrow nor pain of any
70 sort. And Nan and Bet are like to her in this."

      "How old be these?"

      "Fifteen, an' it please you, sir."

      "Thou speakest well; thou hast an easy grace in it. Art learned?"

      "I know not if I am or not, sir. The good priest that is called Father Andrew taught me, of his kindness, from his books."

      "Know'st thou the Latin?"

---

[3] **Offal:** waste or garbage.

The prince
becomes
angry and
upset when
Tom says he is
beaten
at home.

117

2. **REREAD AND CITE TEXT EVIDENCE**

B **ASK STUDENTS** to cite evidence to support their analysis of the prince's character. *Students should cite evidence that the prince scolds the guard and demands that he allow Tom to enter the palace (lines 31–32). From that evidence they may infer that the prince is fair and kind.*

3. **READ AND CITE TEXT EVIDENCE**

C **ASK STUDENTS** to read aloud their description of the prince's reaction to a partner. Have partners work together to find the best evidence to support their descriptions. Have them revise their descriptions if needed. *Students should cite evidence from lines 60–63 to show that the prince becomes angry and upset when Tom says he is beaten at home.*

FOR ELL STUDENTS Students may struggle with some of the vocabulary on this page. Have them work in small groups to discuss the meanings of *thou'st, repast, dost, grand-dam, stayeth, maketh, mayhap, smiteth, sooth, speakest*. Remind them to use context clues to determine the meanings of these words.

"But scantly, sir, I doubt."

"Tell me of thy Offal Court. Hast thou a pleasant life there?"

"In truth, yes, so please you, sir, save when one is hungry. There be
80 Punch-and-Judy[4] shows, and monkeys—oh such antic creatures! and
so bravely dressed!—and there be plays wherein they that play do
shout and fight till all are slain, and 'tis so fine to see, and costeth but
a farthing[5]—albeit 'tis main hard to get the farthing, please your
worship."

(D) "Tell me more."

"We lads of Offal Court do strive against each other with the
cudgel, like to the fashion of the 'prentices, sometimes."

The prince's eyes flashed. Said he—

"Marry, that would not I mislike. Tell me more."

90 "We strive in races, sir, to see who of us shall be fleetest."

"That would I like also. Speak on."

"In summer, sir, we wade and swim in the canals and in the river,
and each doth duck his neighbour, and splatter him with water, and
dive and shout and tumble and—"

"'Twould be worth my father's kingdom but to enjoy it once!
Prithee go on."

"We dance and sing about the Maypole in Cheapside; we play in
the sand, each covering his neighbour up; and times we make mud
pastry—oh the lovely mud, it hath not its like for delightfulness in all
100 the world!—we do fairly wallow in the mud, sir, saving your worship's
presence."

---

[4] **Punch-and-Judy show:** traditional puppet show. The puppets are Mr. Punch and his wife
Judy, who get into comical fights.

[5] **farthing:** a former British coin worth one-fourth of a penny.

---

4. ◄ **REREAD AND DISCUSS** Reread lines 78–111. In a small group,
discuss which elements of Tom's life most appeal to the prince. Cite
text evidence in your discussion.

5. **READ ▶** As you read lines 112–156, continue to cite textual
evidence.

• Underline what the boys realize after they switch clothes.

• Circle what the prince sees on Tom's hand. In the margin, explain the
Prince's reaction.

• In the margin, explain what happens in lines 139–156.

118

"Oh, prithee, say no more, 'tis glorious! If that I could but clothe
me in raiment like to thine, and strip my feet, and revel in the mud
once, just once, with none to rebuke me or forbid, meseemeth I could
forego the crown!"

"And if that I could clothe me once, sweet sir, as thou art clad—
just once—"

"Oho, would'st like it? Then so shall it be. Doff thy rags, and don
these splendours, lad! It is a brief happiness, but will be not less keen
110 for that. We will have it while we may, and change again before any
come to molest."

A few minutes later the little Prince of Wales was garlanded with
Tom's fluttering odds and ends, and the little Prince of Pauperdom
was tricked out in the **gaudy** plumage of royalty. The two went and
stood side by side before a great mirror, and lo, a miracle: there did
not seem to have been any change made! They stared at each other,
then at the glass, then at each other again. At last the puzzled
princeling said—

"What dost thou make of this?"

120 "Ah, good your worship, require me not to answer. It is not meet
that one of my degree should utter the thing."

(F) "Then will *I* utter it. Thou hast the same hair, the same eyes, the
same voice and manner, the same form and stature, the same face and
countenance that I bear. Fared we forth naked, there is none could say
which was you, and which the Prince of Wales. And, now that I am
clothed as thou wert clothed, it seemeth I should be able the more
nearly to feel as thou didst when the brute soldier—Hark ye, is not
this a bruise upon your hand?"

"Yes; but it is a slight thing, and your worship knoweth that the
130 poor man-at-arms—"

(E) "Peace! It was a shameful thing and a cruel!" cried the little
prince, stamping his bare foot. "If the King—Stir not a step till I come
again! It is a command!"

In a moment he had snatched up and put away an article of
national importance that lay upon a table, and was out at the door
and flying through the palace grounds in his bannered rags, with a
hot face and glowing eyes. As soon as he reached the great gate, he
seized the bars, and tried to shake them, shouting—

"Open! Unbar the gates!"

119

The prince
would consider
giving up his
crown if he
could dress
and play like
Tom one time.

gaudy:
flashy; tacky

The prince
sympathizes
with Tom,
especially now
that he is
wearing his
clothes. The
prince sets off
to scold the
guard for
giving Tom a
bruise.

---

4. **REREAD AND DISCUSS USING TEXT EVIDENCE**

(D) **ASK STUDENTS** to appoint a reporter for each group to cite
specific evidence and line numbers to support their conclusions
about which elements of Tom's life most appeal to the prince.
*Students should cite evidence that the prince would like to fight, race,
swim, dance, and wallow in the mud.*

5. **READ AND CITE TEXT EVIDENCE**

(E) **ASK STUDENTS** to cite text evidence to support their
explanation of what happens in lines 131–156. *Students should
cite evidence that the prince is angry: "stamping his bare foot" (line
132), "glowing eyes" (line 137). He is wearing Tom's rags (line 136),
and the soldier struck him, "a sounding box on the ear" (line 142),
having mistaken him for Tom, "'thou beggar's spawn,'" (line 144). The
guard tosses the prince out of the palace (lines 152–153), saying, "'Be
off, thou crazy rubbish!'"*

Critical Vocabulary: gaudy (line 114) Have students
determine the meaning of *gaudy* as it is used here. Is *gaudy* a
compliment? What does this word choice tell you about the
narrator's attitude toward the characters?

FOR ELL STUDENTS Point out to students that *tricked out* (line
114) has nothing to do with playing tricks. It means "adorned,
extravagantly dressed up."

The guard strikes the prince and throws him out of the palace, thinking he is Tom.

mockingly:
in an insulting manner; rudely

140   The soldier that had maltreated Tom obeyed promptly; and as the prince burst through the portal, half-smothered with royal wrath, the soldier fetched him a sounding box on the ear that sent him whirling to the roadway, and said—

     "Take that, thou beggar's spawn, for what thou got'st me from his Highness!"

     The crowd roared with laughter. The prince picked himself out of the mud, and made fiercely at the sentry, shouting—

     "I am the Prince of Wales, my person is sacred; and thou shalt hang for laying thy hand upon me!"

150   The soldier brought his halberd to a present-arms and said **mockingly**—

     "I salute your gracious Highness." Then angrily—"Be off, thou crazy rubbish!"

     Here the jeering crowd closed round the poor little prince, and hustled him far down the road, hooting him, and shouting—

     "Way for his Royal Highness! Way for the Prince of Wales!"

6. ◀ **REREAD**   Reread lines 122–156. How does Tom and the prince's discovery help you understand what happens after the prince leaves Tom? Support your answer with explicit textual evidence.

It explains why the soldier and the crowd treat him badly. They think he is Tom, and again they delight in the mistreatment of a pauper.

SHORT RESPONSE

Cite Text Evidence   Why might the prince want to trade places with Tom? Think about what you know of the prince's character. Review your reading notes and be sure to **cite text evidence** in your response.

The prince is very kind. He is interested in knowing what Tom's life is like—he probably does not have a chance to enjoy being a boy the way Tom does. The prince wants to know what life is like outside the palace—it is not something he experiences, and he realizes that it is the way most people live. He also might want to better understand his future subjects.

120

---

1. **READ** ▶   As you read the introductory text and lines 1–25, begin to collect and cite text evidence.

- Underline details in the setting that suggest royalty.
- Underline stage directions that describe Tom's appearance and behavior.
- Circle the prince's dialogue. In the margin, explain what his response to events tells you about him.

from The Prince and the Pauper
Dramatization by Joellen Bland

CHARACTERS

Edward, Prince of Wales   Two Guards
Tom Canty, the Pauper   Villagers
Two Women

Time: *1547.*

(A) **Setting:** *Westminster Palace, England. Gates leading to courtyard are at right. Slightly to the left, off courtyard and inside gates,* **interior** *of palace anteroom[1] is visible. There is a couch with a rich robe draped on it, screen at rear, bellcord, mirror, chairs, and a table with bowl of nuts, and a large golden seal on it. Piece of armor hangs on one wall. Exits are rear and downstage.*

interior:
inside

Scene One

At Curtain Rise. *Two Guards—one at right, one at left—stand in front of gates, several Villagers hover nearby, straining to see into courtyard where Prince may be seen through fence, playing. Two Women enter right.*

1st Woman. I have walked all morning just to have a glimpse of Westminster Palace.

2nd Woman. Maybe if we can get near enough to the gates, we can have a glimpse of the young Prince. (*Tom Canty,* dirty and ragged, comes out of crowd and steps close to gates.)

10   **Tom.** I have always dreamed of seeing a real prince! (*Excited, he presses his nose against gates.*)

(B)

---

[1] **anteroom:** an outer room that leads to an inner room and is often used as a waiting room.

121

---

6. **REREAD AND CITE TEXT EVIDENCE**

(F) **ASK STUDENTS** to read their response aloud to a partner. Then have partners work together to identify the best evidence. *Answers will vary. Students should cite lines 122–125 as evidence that Tom and the prince look identical, which explains why the soldier treats the prince badly in lines 140–156.*

Critical Vocabulary: mockingly (line 151) Have students model how the word *mockingly* describes the soldier's tone.

SHORT RESPONSE

Cite Text Evidence   Students should:

- provide a text-based analysis of the prince.
- infer the prince's motivations.
- cite textual evidence to support their response.

---

1. **READ AND CITE TEXT EVIDENCE**

(A) **ASK STUDENTS** to explain how they decided which details in the setting suggest royalty. *Students should have underlined these details that suggest the opulence of living in a palace: "Westminster Palace, England. Gates leading to courtyard," "interior of palace anteroom is visible," "couch with a rich robe draped on it," "large golden seal," and "piece of armor."*

Critical Vocabulary: interior (Setting) Ask students to explain why the word *interior* is used to describe the setting. *Students might say that it helps explain the layout of the palace.*

The prince has respect for every one of his countrymen.

1st Guard. Mind your manners, you young beggar! (*Seizes* Tom *by collar and sends him sprawling into crowd.* Villagers *laugh, as* Tom *slowly gets to his feet.*)

Prince (*rushing to gates*). How dare you treat a poor subject of the King in such a manner! Open the gates and let him in! (*As* Villagers *see* Prince, *they take off their hats and bow low.*)

Villagers (*shouting together*). Long live the Prince of Wales! (Guards *open gates and* Tom *slowly passes through, as if in a dream.*)

20 **Prince** (*to* Tom). You look tired, and you have been treated cruelly. I am Edward, Prince of Wales. What is your name?

Tom (*looking around in awe*). Tom Canty, Your Highness.

Prince. Come into the palace with me, Tom. (Prince *leads* Tom *into anteroom.* Villagers *pantomime conversation, and all but a few exit.*) Where do you live, Tom?

Tom. In the city, Your Highness, in Offal Court.

Prince. Offal Court? That's an odd name. Do you have parents?

Tom. Yes, Your Highness.

Prince. How does your father treat you?

30 **Tom.** If it please you, Your Highness, when I am not able to beg a penny for our supper, he treats me to beatings.

Prince (*shocked*). What! Beatings? My father is not a calm man, but he does not beat me. (*looks at* Tom *thoughtfully*) You speak well and have an easy grace. Have you been schooled?

Tom. Very little, Your Highness. A good priest who shares our house in Offal Court has taught me from his books.

2. **◀ REREAD** Reread lines 8–22. In what ways do the stage directions help you understand Tom's character? Cite text evidence in your response.

When he "presses his nose" against the gates and looks "around in awe" we learn he is eager to see the prince and impressed by royalty.

3. **READ ▶** As you read lines 26–48, continue to cite textual evidence.
- Underline what Tom tells the prince about life at Offal Court.
- Circle the stage direction that describes the prince's reaction when he learns that Tom's father hits him.
- In the margin, explain what each character wants.

Prince. Do you have a pleasant life in Offal Court?

Tom. Pleasant enough, Your Highness, save when I am hungry. We have Punch and Judy shows, and sometimes we lads have fights in the 40 street.

Prince (*eagerly*). I should like that. Tell me more.

Tom. In summer, we run races and swim in the river, and we love to wallow in the mud.

Prince (*sighing, wistfully*). If I could wear your clothes and play in the mud just once, with no one to forbid me, I think I could give up the crown!

Tom (*shaking his head*). And if I could wear your fine clothes just once, Your Highness . . .

Prince. Would you like that? Come, then. We shall change places. You 50 can take off your rags and put on my clothes—and I will put on yours. (*He leads* Tom *behind screen, and they return shortly, each wearing the other's clothes.*) Let's look at ourselves in this mirror. (*leads* Tom *to mirror*)

Tom. Oh, Your Highness, it is not proper for me to wear such clothes.

Prince (*excitedly, as he looks in the mirror*). Heavens, do you not see it? We look like brothers! We have the same features and bearing.[2] If we went about together, dressed alike, there is no one who could say which is the Prince of Wales and which is Tom Canty!

Tom (*drawing back and rubbing his hand*). Your Highness, I am 60 frightened. . . .

Prince. Do not worry. (*seeing* Tom *rub his hand*) Is that a bruise on your hand?

Tom. Yes, but it is slight thing, Your Highness.

Prince (*angrily*). It was shameful and cruel of that guard to strike you. Do not stir a step until I come back. I command you! (*He picks up the golden Seal of England[3] and carefully puts it into a piece of armor. He then dashes out to gates.*) Open! Unbar the gates at once! (2nd Guard

[2] **features and bearing:** parts of the face and ways of standing and walking.
[3] **Seal of England:** a device used to stamp a special design, usually a picture of the ruler, onto a document, thus indicating that it has royal approval.

4. **READ ▶** As you read lines 49–79, continue to cite textual evidence.
- In the margin, explain why Tom is "frightened" (line 60).
- Circle how the guards and villagers treat the prince when he leaves the palace in Tom's clothes.

wistfully:
longingly

The prince would love to play in the mud without worry like Tom does. Tom wishes he could wear the prince's clothes.

Tom is afraid of appearing disrespectful by dressing like the prince.

---

2. **REREAD AND CITE TEXT EVIDENCE**

B **ASK STUDENTS** to cite evidence to support their explanation of how the stage directions help them understand Tom's character. *Students should cite "presses his nose against gates" (line 11) and "looking around in awe" (line 22).*

3. **READ AND CITE TEXT EVIDENCE**

C **ASK STUDENTS** to cite text evidence to support their explanation of what Tom and the prince each want. *Students should cite evidence that the prince would love to play in the mud from lines 44–45. They should cite evidence that Tom would like to wear the prince's clothes from lines 47–48.*

4. **READ AND CITE TEXT EVIDENCE**

D **ASK STUDENTS** to use their circled text to explain how the prince is treated differently by the guards and the villagers when he is wearing Tom's clothes. *Students should cite circled text in lines 68–69, 74–77, and 78–79, and explain that the guards and villagers are cruel when they do not recognize the prince.*

Critical Vocabulary: wistfully (line 44) Ask students to explain how the word *wistfully* helps them understand why the prince sighs.

FOR ELL STUDENTS Explain to students that a Punch and Judy show (line 39) is a hand-puppet show featuring a violent man, Punch, and his wife, Judy. Despite the violence, the puppet shows are comedy.

CLOSE READ Notes

D *opens gates, and (as Prince runs out, in rags, 1st Guard seizes him, boxes him on the ear, and knocks him to the ground.)*

70 **1st Guard.** Take that, you little beggar, for the trouble you have made for me with the Prince. *(Villagers roar with laughter.)*
Prince *(picking himself up, turning on Guard furiously).* I am Prince of Wales! You shall hang for laying your hand on me!
1st Guard *(presenting arms; mockingly).* I salute Your Gracious Highness! *(then, angrily, 1st Guard shoves Prince roughly aside.)* Be off, you mad bag of rags! *(Prince is surrounded by Villagers, who hustle him off.)*
E **Villagers** *(ad lib, as they exit, shouting).* Make way for His Royal Highness! Make way for the Prince of Wales! Hail to the Prince! *(Etc.)*

5. ◀ **REREAD AND DISCUSS** Reread lines 1–79. In a small group, discuss how the plot unfolds to create a conflict at the end of this scene. Cite explicit textual evidence in your discussion.

SHORT RESPONSE

Cite Text Evidence How do the stage directions and the dialogue help you understand the characters of Tom and the prince? Be sure to **cite text evidence** in your response.

Tom has a hard life (he is "dirty and ragged"), but he is eager and excited to encounter royalty ("looking around in awe"). The Prince has a good heart ("How dare you treat a poor subject") and reacts against injustice ("shocked"). The stage directions allow the reader to visualize how each person acts ("rushing to gates"). The dialogue also reveals each person's character. For example, the prince shows his kindness ("Open the gates and let him in!") and Tom shows his humility ("And if I could wear your fine clothes just once").

124

CLOSE READ Notes

1. **READ** ▶ As you read the first two pages of the graphic story, begin to collect and cite textual evidence.
• Underline Tom's feelings about the palace and the prince.
• Circle text that shows the prince's character.

from **The Prince and the Pauper**
Graphic Story by Marvel Comics

125

---

5. **REREAD AND DISCUSS USING TEXT EVIDENCE**

E **ASK STUDENTS** to be prepared to share the results of their discussion with the class. Have them appoint a reporter for each group. *Students should cite evidence of Tom's curiosity (lines 10–11), the prince's kindness (lines 20–21), and the two boys' appearance (lines 55–56).*

SHORT RESPONSE

Cite Text Evidence Student responses will vary, but they should cite evidence from the text to support their explanation. Students should:

• explain how stage directions give insight into Tom and the prince.
• explain how dialogue gives insight into Tom and the prince.
• cite textual evidence to support their response.

1. **READ AND CITE TEXT EVIDENCE**

A **ASK STUDENTS** to use their marked text to describe how Tom feels about the palace and the prince. *Students should underline text in the fourth panel: "Was the desire of his soul to be satisfied at last?" and explain that Tom wants very much to see the prince. They should underline text in the fifth panel: "a spectacle that almost made him shout for joy," and explain that Tom is happy to see the prince.*

The jagged
outlines show
forceful
expression—
the prince is
outraged.

I strike you
because you
got me in
trouble with
the prince.
Now go away!

2. **REREAD** Reread the page above. How do the illustrations convey that the boys look alike? Circle illustrations that help you recognize their similarities.

The illustrations show that the boys have similar facial features.
They also appear to be the same height and have the same build. The
boys are frequently drawn side by side so that we can see that they
are very much alike.

126

3. **READ** As you read this page, continue to cite textual evidence.

• Circle the dialogue that is shown with jagged outlines. In the margin, explain why the artist has used these outlines.
• In the margin, paraphrase what the guard says to the prince.
• Circle the prince's facial expression in the last panel.

127

2. REREAD AND CITE TEXT EVIDENCE

B **ASK STUDENTS** which illustrations they circled and what similarities they noticed in those illustrations. *Students may indicate that the oval illustration and the illustration at the right in the bottom row show that the boys have similar facial features, hair, and similar builds. They should conclude that the boys are drawn side by side so that readers can see that they look very much alike.*

FOR ELL STUDENTS The word *duck* has several meanings. As a noun it can describe a water bird and as a verb it can mean "to lower or to evade." In this context, though, it means "to push under water."

3. READ AND CITE TEXT EVIDENCE

C **ASK STUDENTS** to use their marked text as evidence and describe the feelings the prince experiences on this page. *Students should circle the jagged speech bubble in panel 1 on this page. They should explain that this shows that the prince is angry. They should see that the prince looks stunned when the guard abuses him. They should circle the prince's expression in the last panel, and explain that he is feeling sad and afraid.*

4. ◀ **REREAD AND DISCUSS** The only time we see the prince's reaction to being thrown out is in the graphic story. In a small group, discuss how learning the prince's reaction impacts your perception of events.

SHORT RESPONSE

Cite Text Evidence Analyze the way you learn about Tom and the prince's similarities in the three versions of the story. Which version was most effective? Review your reading notes and **cite text evidence** in your response.

Possible response: It is easy to see what the characters are feeling in a graphic story. Tom looks longingly through the bars, and is happy to see the prince. The prince is very upset when the guard hits him as he leaves the palace. It is apparent that the two boys are identical, and that they strike up an immediate friendship. The speech bubbles show if they are shouting and are upset. In the final panel, the prince realizes what life is like for a pauper, as he is brutally beaten by his own guard.

128

---

4. **REREAD AND DISCUSS USING TEXT EVIDENCE** Have students review the ending of each version.

D **ASK STUDENTS** to cite text evidence to support their analysis of how learning the prince's reaction impacts the reader's perception of events. *Students should cite the final panel as evidence that the prince is sad and afraid. They may say that this ending is sadder than the other two.*

SHORT RESPONSE

Cite Text Evidence Student responses will vary, but they should cite evidence from the text to support their analysis. Students should:

- analyze characterizations in all three versions.
- determine which version most effectively showed the similarities between Tom and the prince.
- cite textual evidence to support their response.

TO CHALLENGE STUDENTS . . .

Students will benefit from comparing and contrasting the experience of reading a drama to hearing it read aloud as a reader's theater performance or seeing it acted out. First, invite students to reread Joellen Bland's dramatization of *The Prince and the Pauper*, paying special attention to what they "see" or "hear" in their minds as they are reading. Then, work with students to prepare a performance of the script.

Assign students the parts of Prince Edward, Tom Canty, Two Women, Two Guards, and Villagers. You may also assign a stage director to read the stage directions. For more historical context, students may research the Tudor period of British history, and Prince Edward VI. Students may set the stage with simple props or designs that evoke the period of the scene.

ASK STUDENTS in the audience to contrast what they "see" and "hear" in their minds when they are reading the text to what they perceive when they listen or watch. After the performance, discuss as a class the differences between reading a drama and seeing or hearing it.

DIG DEEPER

1. With the class, return to novel excerpt Question 6, Reread, on page 120. Have students share their responses.

ASK STUDENTS to cite the text evidence that led to their understanding of what happens after the prince leaves Tom.

- Ask students what Tom and the prince discover in lines 122–125. *Students should say that Tom and the prince discover that they look alike.*

- Have students cite text that shows that Tom and the prince look alike. *Students may identify "none could say which was you, and which the Prince of Wales" (lines 124–125).*

- Have students cite text that shows that the prince left Tom. *Students may cite lines 134–136, "In a moment he…was out at the door and flying through the palace grounds…."*

- Have students paraphrase what happens after the prince leaves Tom. *Possible answer: The prince demands that the soldier who bullied Tom unbar the gate. The prince thinks he is going to yell at the soldier, but instead the soldier hits him, and the villagers laugh at him. Then the soldier kicks the prince off the palace grounds.*

- Ask students why the soldier did not recognize the prince. *The prince looked exactly like Tom, once he was wearing Tom's clothes.*

2. With the class, return to drama Question 5, Reread and Discuss, on page 124. Have students share their responses.

ASK STUDENTS whether they were satisfied with the outcome of their small-group discussions. Have each group share their conclusions about how the plot unfolds to create a conflict at the end of the scene. What evidence did the group cite in the discussion?

- Ask students to share personal insights that were not reported with the conclusions of the group. What evidence supported their personal conclusions?

- As a class, draft a written response to Question 5 that is composed of the most compelling conclusions reported by groups and individuals. Demonstrate how to support conclusions with evidence from the text.

ASK STUDENTS to return to their Short Response answer and revise it based on the class discussion.

CLOSE READING NOTES

Acknowledgments

Index of Titles & Authors